KIERKEGAARD

within your grasp™

170301

By Shelley O'Hara

WILEY

Wiley Publishing, Inc.

Kierkegaard Within Your Grasp™

Copyright © 2004 Wiley, Hoboken, NJ

Published by:

Wiley Publishing, Inc.

111 River Street

Hoboken, NJ 07030-5774

www.wiley.com

Published simultaneously in Canada

Cataloguing-in-Publication Data available from the Library of Congress.

Library of Congress Control Number: 2004101615

ISBN: 0-7645-5974-5

1O/QS/QW/QU/IN

Manufactured in the United States of America

10 9 8 7 6 5 4 3 2 1

Table of Contents

Acknowledgments

A bouquet of thanks to Cindy Kitchel for suggesting me for this project. A round of applause and cheers to Greg Tubach, Acquisitions Editor; Elizabeth Kuball, Project Editor Extraordinaire; and Dave Stout, Technical Editor and Philosophy Scholar.

Kierkegaard's Life

What is truth but to live for an idea
—Søren Kierkegaard

There's no question that Kierkegaard's life had an impact on his thinking and his writing. His father's influence, his engagement to and subsequent break from his fiancée, his religious upbringing, and other factors all play an integral role in his works. In addition to a fuller understanding, such considerations often provide insight into their mistakes as well as their successes. A good understanding of Kierkegaard's life, his education, and his goals prepares you for reading and comprehending his writings.

As the Father, So the Son

Søren Kierkegaard (pronounced *Sir*-ren *Keer*-ker-gaw, *Keer*-ker-gore, or *Keer*-ca-guard) was born in Copenhagen, Denmark, on May 5, 1813, the youngest of seven children. His father, Michael, was poor as a child, lived in a small village, and tended sheep. Even the origin of the Kierkegaard surname came from Michael's relationship to the church. As an indentured laborer for the church (Kirke), he was provided a portion of the church's farm (Gaard) for his family's use.

When Michael was 12 years old, he was sent to live with his uncle, a prosperous tradesman. Michael received an education and established himself in trade, becoming wealthy enough to retire at the age of 40 and spend the rest of his life at leisure.

After his first wife died, Michael Kierkegaard married Anne Lund, a domestic servant who was pregnant with their first child at the time of their marriage. Anne eventually bore all seven of the Kierkegaard children. Søren Kierkegaard writes little of his mother, and little is known about her. She has been described as cheerful and motherly, as well as illiterate.

Kierkegaard's father's upbringing is significant for several reasons. Michael came from a thrifty, pious congregation, with very strict ideas of sin and suffering. Focused on this sin and suffering, Michael Kierkegaard doubted the salvation of his soul and suffered from depression. He was well read and liked to discuss spiritual matters with his son Søren. Michael's outlook on life was based on guilt, punishment, and hardship, and he reared his seven children with this same worldview.

As a child, Michael Kierkegaard had suffered cold and hardship on the farm, enough so that he cursed God. Because he had offended God, Michael believed that he had cursed his family, and his children would not live beyond the age of 34 (like Christ, who was crucified at 33). Although Michael lived to 82, only two of his seven children (one of them Søren) lived past the age of 34, and Søren Kierkegaard felt the burden of this "curse."

From his father, Søren Kierkegaard inherited his worldview, his lifelong melancholy, and his love of reading and penetrating discussion, as the following passage from Kierkegaard's journals indicates:

It was all connected with the relationship with my father, the person I have loved the most—and what does that mean? It means that he is just the person who makes one miserable—but out of love.

Kierkegaard Seeks His Path

At the age of 17, Kierkegaard enrolled in the University of Copenhagen and studied theology. He also read and studied philosophy and *aesthetics,* the branch of philosophy that deals with art and artistic judgment. Kierkegaard's first major philosophical work, *Either/Or,* deals with this topic. (You can read more about *Either/Or* in Chapter 3.)

Kierkegaard enjoyed university life, attending plays, the opera, and parties, and running up debt, which he relied on his father to repay. At least on the surface, Søren Kierkegaard appeared to enjoy the somewhat frivolous and directionless life of a permanent student.

Kierkegaard's outward life of fun hid a growing sense of dissatisfaction over the emptiness of his life. In his journals, he likens himself to the two-faced Janus—one face laughs, the other face cries. He seemed to struggle trying to find, as he wrote in his journals, "the idea I will live and die for." In an effort to find himself, Kierkegaard took a vacation to Gilleleje, a coastal resort. The following journal writing gives a glimpse of his struggle:

What I really need is to come to terms with myself about what I am to do. . . . It is a matter of understanding my destiny, of seeing what the Divinity actually wants me to do; what counts is to find a truth, which is true for me.

This desire to find his calling became even more urgent when Kierkegaard's father, Michael, died in 1838. Kierkegaard interpreted his father's death as a sacrifice. Søren Kierkegaard writes in his journals, "[H]e had died for me, so that, if possible, something might still be made of me." After his father's death, Kierkegaard returned to his studies and was awarded a degree in theology in 1840, graduating magna cum laude.

Love (Or Not) for Kierkegaard

During his years at the University of Copenhagen, Kierkegaard met and began a courtship with Regine Olsen. In 1840, they became engaged. Kierkegaard's relationship with Regine, like the one with his father, greatly influenced his outlook and writings.

Although he loved Regine deeply, Kierkegaard knew that his melancholy would adversely affect a marriage, and he didn't want to ruin Regine's happy life with his ever-present sense of sadness and gloom. (There are other interpretations of his reasons for breaking the engagement, but this is the one Kierkegaard gave and most scholars highlight.) Because he did not think he could overcome his bouts of depression, and because he also did not think that he could confide in Regine about his depression, he immediately had doubts about the engagement. He wrote in his journal:

If I had not had my vita ante acta [my melancholy], if I had not had my depression—marriage to her would have made me happier than I had ever dreamed of becoming. But being the person I unfortunately am, I must say that I could become happier in my unhappiness without her than with her.

Because a broken engagement at this period in Denmark could reflect unfavorably on both people, but especially the woman, Kierkegaard sought to find a way to break the engagement in such a way that the act would be blamed on him rather than her. To make it seem as though Regine was the one to break the engagement, he acted the part of a philandering bachelor. Regine saw through his actions, however, and refused to break off the engagement herself. After much heartache, Kierkegaard finally ended the engagement himself in 1841. He wrote in his journal, "And so we parted.

I spent the whole night crying on my bed. . . . I went to Berlin. I suffered greatly. I thought of her every day."

His relationship with Regine affected Kierkegaard, not only personally, but philosophically. Themes relating to his decision and sacrifice are prevalent in his work. Regine later became engaged and married Fredrich Schlegel in 1847. Kierkegaard changed the ending to *The Repetition,* the book he was about to publish when he heard about the engagement. In the original manuscript, the hero is distraught after his loved one becomes engaged to another and commits suicide. The new conclusion has the hero taking a different approach to the news; he feels a release from the burden and proclaims his joy:

> I am myself again; the machinery has been started up. Cut are the meshes I was ensnared in; broken is the spell that had me bewitched. . . . I belong to the idea. When it beckons me, I follow it and when it makes an appointment I wait days and nights; there none calls me to dinner, there none waits with supper. When the idea calls I leave everything; or rather, I have nothing to leave; I betray no one, I grieve no one by being true. . . . When I return home, no one reads in my look; no one questions my appearance; no one demands of my manner an explanation. . . . The cup of intoxication is handed back to me. Already I breathe in its fragrance; already I sense its effervescent music. . . . Long live the flight of thought; long live danger in the service of the idea . . . long live the dance in the whirl of the infinite . . . long live the wave that hurls me up above the stars.

Kierkegaard Publishes Profusely

His broken engagement to Regine was a turning point in Kierkegaard's life; it was the beginning of Kierkegaard's extensive writing career. Kierkegaard threw himself into his work and throughout his life enjoyed a monastic devotion to his calling. His lack of any close, personal relationships with women enabled him to admire and idealize them from afar. He lived as a wealthy bachelor off of the inheritance he received from his father. Although he received income from his writing, his financial security was never an issue, and it's unlikely that financial success was what drove him to publish so prodigiously in his short life.

Although Kierkegaard had considered and prepared for a career in the ministry, he was never ordained. (His elder brother followed a similar course of studies and did become an ordained minister. He was the only sibling other than Søren who lived past the age of 34.) He did preach sermons and play an active role in criticizing and seeking to reform the Christian Church, especially and more directly in his later life.

Kierkegaard had a unique publishing tactic; he wrote and published under various pseudonyms, in addition to publishing under his own name. It wasn't anonymity that drove his decision, but instead a unique literary strategy that he used to further his messages. (You can read more about his use of pseudonyms in Chapter 2.)

In addition to his philosophy and religious writings, Kierkegaard also wrote literary criticism, sermons, and reviews.

During his lifetime, Kierkegaard wrote profusely, sometimes publishing two works within a few weeks of each other. Chapter 2 covers the writing, publication, and reception of Kierkegaard's works.

Kierkegaard Takes On . . .

Kierkegaard spent his entire life in Copenhagen. He traveled outside Denmark to Berlin only a few times. He mostly attended the theater, wrote, and walked about the city.

Two significant life events worth noting include his tangle with the press (often referred to as the *Corsair* Affair in writings about Kierkegaard); this event happened at the start of his writing career. The other event, a direct attack on the Church, occurred at the end of his life.

The Press

Even though Kierkegaard wrote under a pseudonym and didn't come out officially with his authorship until later in his career, his identity as the author of the works he published was well known in the literary circles of the time. In 1845, a highly regarded critic, P. L. Møller, wrote a review of Kierkegaard's works. Although most of the review was positive, Møller did write some scathing remarks—remarks that were more of a personal comment on Kierkegaard's life and engagement fiasco than a critique of his writing.

Kierkegaard knew and probably disliked Møller even before the review, but after the review he was angry. He knew that Møller wrote for *The Corsair*, a satirical weekly paper that ridiculed popular people in Copenhagen, and he retaliated by revealing Møller's connection to *The Corsair*. He also challenged *The Corsair* to include him in its selection of victims for ridicule.

Although he probably didn't intend for this challenge to be taken literally, it was.

The editor of *The Corsair* responded and what followed was a long and bitter attack on Kierkegaard and his personal habits. Prior to this, Kierkegaard liked to walk around Copenhagen and talked frequently with common people he met. He was also generous to beggars. After the pieces appeared in *The Corsair*, people ridiculed him on the street, and he didn't feel comfortable walking around. "Even the butcher's boy almost thinks himself justified in being offensive to me at the behest of *The Corsair*," he wrote in his journals. In addition to his friendly and generous nature, Kierkegaard had a crooked and sway back; his legs were thin, and he walked strangely. In the satire, he was drawn in various caricatures, picking on his physical problems. Kierkegaard was humiliated by these publications, and he suffered greatly.

The *Corsair* Affair had a direct effect on Kierkegaard's writing. In his personal journal writings and his philosophical work, the role of suffering in one's life is a key theme.

The Danish People's Church

One other life event worth mentioning is the pamphlet attack he led near the end of his life against the Church.

The Lutheran Church in Denmark was a State Church; being a citizen of Denmark also meant enrollment into the Lutheran Church. Kierkegaard was incensed by the lack of involvement it took to be a Christian, and he felt that "Official Christianity" or "Christendom" had departed so far from the New Testament teachings that it needed to be torn down and rebuilt. It's important to note that Kierkegaard was a believer; he was not attacking the teachings of Christianity, but the official way it was sanctioned and carried out by the Lutheran Church at the time. His feelings about the church came to a head after the death of a prominent bishop, J. P. Mynster.

Mynster was a friend of Kierkegaard's father, so Kierkegaard knew him personally. Despite the connection to his father, Kierkegaard's opinion of Mynster grew less favorable. Basically, Kierkegaard thought the bishop lived a life that was too comfortable, too materialistic, too urbane—a contrast to living with real Christian values.

When the popular bishop died, H. L. Martensen, a professor of theology and one of Kierkegaard's professors, wrote and published a memorial sermon. In this sermon, Martensen referred to Mynster as one of the true witnesses of the Christian Church. Kierkegaard used this expression (true witness, a witness to the truth) to describe the true Christian, the martyr, and he became incensed when Martensen used it to refer to Mynster.

Kierkegaard began publishing a series of pamphlets, under his own name, using his own money. He also changed his writing style and addressed his audience directly in this journal that he named *The Instant*. He sought to renew Christian faith within the church. Kierkegaard was profoundly religious and greatly influenced by Martin Luther and Luther's attack on Catholic doctrine that was not supported by scripture. He was clearly hoping for an analogous reformation within the Danish People's Church of the time. His aims are summed up in this excerpt from "Introduction to the Philosopher" by Frithiof Brandt and Peter P. Rohde, at the Kierkegaard on the Internet Web site (www.webcom.com/kierke):

> He spoke in his own name, not in order to rebuke the Church and the clergy for not fulfilling the strict demands of Christianity (for he was well aware that neither they nor he could do that), but because, while they failed, they refused to admit that they neither could nor would conform to the demands, preferring to live in domestic comfort and prosperity and worldly culture, while trying to make themselves and the world believe that this was the meaning of Christianity.

Kierkegaard wrote nine issues of *The Instant* and was readying the tenth when he fell ill.

An Early Death

According to recent analysis of his hospital records, Kierkegaard probably suffered from progressive spinal paralysis. In October of 1855, after a fall in the street, he was taken to Frederiks Hospital. He died November 11, 1855, at the age of 42.

Søren Kierkegaard is buried in the Kierkegaard family burial place in Copenhagen, and this hymnal verse appears on his original gravestone:

> There is a little time,
> Then have I won,
> Then will the entire strife
> Be suddenly gone,
> Then can I rest
> In halls of roses
> And ceaselessly [with]
> My Jesus speak.

This original tombstone, in fact, now resides in the Copenhagen City Museum. His grave now contains a newer stone with a shortened version of this verse.

Kierkegaard's work remained in obscurity until it was read and promoted by Georg Brandes, a Danish critic. Kierkegaard's fame then quickly spread through Germany, Scandinavia, and France, as well as to the United States. Kierkegaard would most likely not have been surprised; he wrote with that goal in mind and noted in his journal, during the *Corsair* Affair, "To my contemporaries my significance depends on my trousers; it may be that to a later era my significance will also depend a little on my writings."

Kierkegaard's Philosophy

I am a poet. But I was made for religion long before I became a poet.

—Søren Kierkegaard

Often referred to as the Father of Existentialism, Kierkegaard's life directly influenced his philosophy. (His life is covered in more detail in Chapter 1.) This chapter covers his major themes, the issues he addressed, who influenced him, the purpose of his writing, how his philosophy evolved during his life, and the relevance of his writings today.

Modern Philosophy's Quest for Answers

Understanding what issues philosophers were grappling with during this time is helpful in understanding Kierkegaard. The prevailing worldview had been influenced by science and rationalism, and philosophers were reacting to how this new reliance on science for all answers affected the more traditional views.

Kierkegaard wrote at a defining point in the history of philosophy. Philosophy students would call him a *counter-Enlightenment writer.* That is, he was reacting to what he saw as problems created by the worldview that was the Enlightenment. The Enlightenment movement, in the 17th and 18th centuries, sought to combine the prevailing concepts of God, nature, knowledge, and man into a cohesive worldview. Enlightenment thinkers emphasized reason and its use to understand and better life.

Rather than knowledge of humanity being gained through systematic rational philosophy or reason, Kierkegaard held that human beings are not primarily creatures of reason or rationality but caring, desiring, and feeling beings that act and make decisions based on this nature. This, by the way, is the heart of Existentialism (described later in this chapter).

Philosophers during both periods sought to answer the following questions:

- What is knowledge? How can we know anything outside our own minds? What is the source of knowledge?

- What is truth? How can something be proved? (The rationalists believed that some things—for instance, mathematical concepts— just "are." A person did not have to experience these things for them to be true. On the flip side, empiricists thought that knowledge must be validated by experience.)

- Is truth objective (universal) or subjective (the truth for an individual, varying from one person to the next)?

- How do science and God relate? Is there a God? If so, how do we know there is one? And how can we prove there is one?

- How are mind and body related? Are they separate things or the same thing?

- What is free will? Are our actions predetermined? That is, do they follow from the preceding action in accordance with the laws of nature? Or do we, indeed, have a choice? How "free" are we?

Kierkegaard addressed many of these issues in his writing, in particular his response to his contemporary and the philosophical theory of the time, Hegelianism.

Kierkegaard Responds to Hegel

G. W. F. Hegel (1770–1831) created a philosophy widely respected during his time, in which he sought to determine the status of religious beliefs. He wanted to reconcile religion and reason and, in so doing, prove that all the fundamental beliefs of Christianity could be shown to be objectively true. Hegel created a philosophical system that, in his eyes, encompassed all thought. He wanted to show that there were universal truths that could be discovered and that these truths were based on opposing ideas. He even went so far as to rank the angels in importance.

Kierkegaard disagreed in this assessment of knowledge and the role of religion versus science. For Kierkegaard, religion was a matter of faith, not reason. His other major criticism of Hegel was that this system was abstracted from everyday life; it was written from outside the system. Kierkegaard believed that, because man has a beginning and an end, because existence is incomplete and constantly changing, and because man must exist within the system he created, the system could not be all-encompassing.

Kierkegaard also sought to stress the individual and his role in making choices based on his own convictions rather than an accepted path. He writes in *A Literary Review:*

> In fact there are handbooks for everything, and very soon education, all the world over, will consist in learning a greater or lesser number of comments by heart, and people will excel according to their capacity of singling out the various facts like a printer singling out the letter, but completely ignorant of the meaning of anything.

Kierkegaard's ideas became the groundwork for a philosophy that came to be called Existentialism.

The Father of Existentialism

Kierkegaard has been called the Father of Existentialism, although he rarely used that term in his writing and, when he did, the term did not have the same meaning as it does today. The term Existentialism has changed considerably over time and even still continues to evolve.

Existentialism is a life-view in which the individual creates his own system of ethics through his choices and in which the individual is ultimately responsible for his actions. For a person who believes in God, as Kierkegaard did, the individual is responsible, ultimately before God. For an atheist, the individual does not have a framework of morality based on an ultimate judging deity.

The *Dictionary of Philosophy* lists these common and accepted aspects of Existentialism:

- Existence precedes Essence. Forms do not determine existence to be what it is. Existence fortuitously becomes and is whatever it becomes and is, and that existence then makes up its "essence."

- An individual has no essential nature, no self-identity other than that involved in the act of choosing.

- Truth is subjectivity.

- Abstractions can never grasp nor communicate the reality of individual existence.

- Philosophy must concern itself with the human nothingness, anticipation of death.

- The universe has no rational direction or scheme. It is meaningless and absurd.

- The universe does not provide moral rules. Moral principles are constructed by humans in the context of being responsible for their actions and for the actions of others.

- Individual actions are unpredictable.

- Individuals have complete freedom of the will.

- Individuals cannot help but make choices.

- An individual can become completely other than what he is.

Themes in Kierkegaard's Work

Kierkegaard's religious outlook was greatly influenced by his father, and his religious view concerned itself with sin, guilt, suffering, and individual responsibility. These themes and Kierkegaard's reaction to these concepts are prevalent in his work.

Kierkegaard's philosophy was based on a call or challenge to how to be a Christian in Christendom. In his writings, he offered his readers thoughtful and profound scenarios for discovering these truths.

How Should Life Be Lived?

Kierkegaard's first work, *Either/Or,* addresses the idea of how to approach life. In this work, Kierkegaard presents two lifestyles: aesthetic and ethical.

He defines the *aesthetic* as someone who is immersed in sensuous experiences, someone who values possibility over actuality, and someone whose main role in life is to avoid boredom. This person enjoys art, literature, and music and is represented by various fictional characters as well as characters from literature (in particular Don Juan) in *Either/Or.*

Kierkegaard contrasts this life-view with that of the *ethical* person, represented by the Judge in *Either/Or.* This person feels a duty to God, country, and mankind. When faced with making a decision, this person looks inward and ponders the correct ethical action seriously. This person consciously chooses instead of responding to a situation; in making his decision, he applies moral codes or rules.

Kierkegaard thought that when a person let choices be made for him (as in the aesthetic lifestyle), he felt despair. And he thought that the avoidance of despair could motivate the aesthetic person to move beyond that lifestyle by making a commitment to the ethical life. That is, a person could change his life if motivated.

In *Stages on Life's Way,* Kierkegaard adds a third stage—religious—to this progression:

> The aesthetic sphere is the sphere of immediacy, the ethical the sphere of requirement (and this requirement is so infinite that the individual always goes bankrupt), the religious the sphere of fulfillment, but, please note, not a fulfillment such as when one fills an alms box or a sack of gold, for repentance has specifically created a boundless space, and as a consequence the religious contraction: simultaneously to be out on 70,000 fathoms of water and yet be joyful.

For the religious person, good and evil does not depend on social norms but on God. A person must decide issues for himself based on religious faith.

Note that Kierkegaard did not believe people shouldn't enjoy the finer pleasures of life; he most certainly did himself. He simply thought that pleasure should not be the motivating factor in one's life.

How Can You Know God?

Kierkegaard discussed the paradox of religion and, hence, why reason or logic could not be used to prove the existence of God or understand God. The central paradox was Jesus, the eternal God becoming human. Kierkegaard proposed that a person could have two reactions to this paradox. He could take offense or he could have faith. If the person chose faith, he had to suspend reason and believe in something higher.

What Is Faith?

Many of Kierkegaard's works deal with the issue of faith and how Kierkegaard defines it. Kierkegaard believed that a person must make a leap from unbelief to belief and that this leap was made on faith. He thought that faith was a miracle, a gift from God, and that, through faith, a person might find eternal truth.

Faith was not a one-time deal. One doesn't just choose faith once; one must constantly choose and renew faith. Kierkegaard defined *faith* as the opposite of sin. With faith, we can atone for our sins. With faith, one becomes his true self, and it is this self that God will judge; hence Kierkegaard's emphasis on faith.

Also, Kierkegaard used the concept of "virtue of the absurd" in many of his works. What he means by this is the paradoxical notion that only the absurd is the "reasonable" choice, since reason must be suspended and subjective passion embraced when dealing with issues such as faith.

The Importance of the Individual

You can see the emergence of existential thought in Kierkegaard's emphasis on the individual. Kierkegaard focused on man's relationship to God. He thought that God had no relation to mankind as a whole, but that God was concerned with the individual. The individual couldn't get by with just blindly repeating church dogma, and his relationship with God was not mediated by clergy, by traditions, or by religion itself. Instead, everything boiled down to the individual before God.

Kierkegaard thought that being an individual was especially difficult for the well-educated and feared it was too easy to become a stereotyped member of the "crowd." He thought it was important for the individual to discover and fulfill his own unique identity and to do so making responsible choices. As he wrote in *Either/Or:*

> For although there is only one situation in which either/or has absolute significance, namely when truth, righteousness, and holiness are lined up on one side, and lust and base propensities and obscure passions and perdition on the other; yet it is always important to choose rightly, even as between things which one may innocently choose; it is important to test oneself, lest some day one might have to beat a retreat to the point from which one started, and might have reason to thank God if one had to reproach oneself for nothing worse than a waste of time.

The Sacrifice for a Higher Good

The concept of sacrifice also plays an important role in Kierkegaard's work. Sacrifice was especially relevant to Kierkegaard's view of his relationships with his father and Regine, his one-time fiancée. He explored the idea of sacrifice of worldly happiness for a higher (religious) purpose. Throughout his life, he questioned the sacrifices he had made. He looked also at the Biblical sacrifices, most notably, the story of Abraham and Isaac, the basis for *Fear and Trembling*. He challenged his readers to realize and live up to the challenges of living a truly Christian life.

How Can One Be a Christian in Christendom?

In the end, Kierkegaard's writing dealt with this key problem: how to become a Christian in Christendom. All his works present solutions and approaches to this problem, and his later works deal explicitly with this topic.

Kierkegaard's Work

Kierkegaard was a prolific writer and used a unique writing style to challenge his readers to think for themselves. He published his most well-known and well-read works using a variety of pseudonyms, but he also published using his own name (mostly sermonic essays). This section covers his writing style, as well as provides a list of his works and summarizes the most important of them.

Kierkegaard's Writing Style

Inspired by Socrates, Kierkegaard wanted readers to abandon any pat stereotypical answers and to force the readers to think for themselves. In his writing, he does not speak directly to the reader, but instead he presents a variety of characters who speak from their own point of view. Kierkegaard felt that essays were unimaginative and dialog was more vivid and personal. He wanted to avoid preaching to his readers. His style, instead, invites the reader to view things from each character's viewpoint and draw his or her own conclusions.

This writing style can make reading Kierkegaard difficult, because the reader has to remember who is talking. A character presenting a particular point of view? Kierkegaard? A "set-up" character used to prove an argument incorrect? Kierkegaard's writing can also be taken out of context; just because a character presents a particular point of view does not mean that Kierkegaard agrees with that view. Kierkegaard cautions the reader himself in this journal entry:

> My authorship has two parts: one pseudonymous and the other signed. The pseudonymous writers are poetized personalities, poetically maintained so that everything they say is in character with their poetized individualities. . . . Anyone with just a fragment of common sense will perceive that it would be ludicrously confusing to attribute to me everything the poetized characters say.

Kierkegaard is also clever in his use of pseudonyms. He used names such as Victor Eremita ("the victorious hermit") and Johannes Climacus, the name of a Greek monk who wrote a book called *Ladder of Paradise*. Both of these names are pertinent to the work. In late writings, the pseudonymous writer opposed to Johannes Climacus was "Anti-Climacus." The reader might appreciate that irony, and the reference hints at the depth of Kierkegaard's literary effort. Kierkegaard also uses names within his works that provide additional literary references.

Kierkegaard's Pseudonymous Writing

A timeline of Kierkegaard's work illustrates how prolific he was. He published major works often, sometimes within days of each other. Also, some works continue themes presented in an earlier work. For instance, *Stages on Life's Way* continues the discussion of approaches to life presented in *Either/Or*. Ideas presented in *Philosophical Fragments* are more fully explored in *The Concluding Unscientific Postscript;* both are written using the same pseudonym.

The following table provides a list of Kierkegaard's publications, publication date, and the pseudonym used.

Work	Publication Date	Pseudonym Used
Either/Or	February 1843	Victor Eremita (the victorious hermit), the editor
		A, editor/author of Part One (Either)
		B, Judge Williams, editor/author of Part Two (Or)

Work	Publication Date	Pseudonym Used
Repetition	October 1843	Constantin Constantius
Fear and Trembling	October 1843	Johannes de Silentio ("silence")
Philosophical Fragments	June 1844	Johannes Climacus
The Concept of Dread (Anxiety)	June 1844	Vigilius Haufniensis ("alert or watchful Copenhager")
Prefaces	June 1844	Nicholaus Notabene
Stages on Life's Way	April 1845	Hilarious Bookbinder, editor
		Afham, author of first section
		Frater Taciturnus, author of third section
The Concluding Unscientific Postscript	February 1846	Johannes Climacus
The Crisis	1848	Inter et Inter ("between and between")
Two Minor Ethical-Religious Essays	1849	HH
The Sickness Unto Death	July 1849	Anti-Climacus
Training in Christianity	September 1850	Anti-Climacus

Kierkegaard's Signed Writing

In addition to his pseudonymous writings, Kierkegaard also wrote many essays that he published under his own name. Many of these works were published simultaneously or in close proximity to his other works.

Also, many of his signed writings take the format of a sermon (Kierkegaard did not feel he had the authority to preach, so he did not call them sermons). In these "edifying works," Kierkegaard seeks to uplift (edify) the individual in faith. Section titles within the discourses—"Every Good and Every Perfect Gift Is from Above," "Purity of Heart Is to Will One Thing," and "Love Shall Hide the Multitude of Sins"—give a good sense of their content.

Note that, later in his career, Kierkegaard dropped the use of his pseudonyms and wrote directly to his audience. Some of these later works include "Works of Love," "On My Work as an Author," and his writing on the attack upon Christendom.

His signed writings include the following:

- "Two Edifying Discourses" (published in May 1843)

- "Three Edifying Discourses" (published in October 1843)

- "Four Edifying Discourses" (published in December 1843)

- "Two Edifying Discourses" (published in March 1844)

- "Three Edifying Discourses" (published in June 1844)

- "Four Edifying Discourses" (published in August 1844)

- "Three Discourses on Imagined Occasions" (published in April 1845)

- "Eighteen Edifying Discourses" (published in May 1845)

- "A Literary Review" (published in March 1846)

- "Edifying Discourses in Various Spirits" (published in March 1847)

- "Works of Love" (published in September 1847)

- "Christian Discourses" (published in April 1848)

- "The Lily of the Field" and "The Birds of the Air" (both published in May 1849)

- "Three Discourses at the Communion on Friday" (published in November 1849)

- "An Edifying Discourse" (published in December 1850)

- "On My Work as an Author" (published in August 1851)

- "Two Discourses at the Communion on Fridays" (published in August 1851)

- "For Self-Examination" (published in September 1851)

- "Judge for Yourself" (written in 1851, published posthumously in 1876)

- "Christ's Judgment on Official Christianity" (published in June 1855)

- "The Unchangeableness of God" (published in September 1855)

- *The Instant* (published as a series of pamphlets throughout 1855)

A Brief Explanation of Kierkegaard's Major Works

Later chapters in this book delve into some of Kierkegaard's major works, including *Either/Or, The Concept of Dread, Fear and Trembling,* and *The Concluding Unscientific Postscript.* The following list offers short summaries of all his major works:

- *Either/Or* marks the start of Kierkegaard's prolific writing career and is his longest work. This piece presents and contrasts two styles of living: the aesthetic and the ethical. The aesthetic person is concerned with sensory pleasure and lives for the moment. The ethical person bases his life on moral codes and is concerned with the eternal. You can read more about this work in Chapter 3.

- *Fear and Trembling* is concerned with the concept of faith and uses the story of Abraham and Isaac to explore the issue. Kierkegaard, in this work, presents the viewpoint that, because religion is so paradoxical, there may be times in which religion can conflict with the ethical demands defined by society. For a more complete description of this work, turn to Chapter 4.

- *Repetition* is an extension of *Fear and Trembling* and treats faith psychologically. The subtitle of this work is "An essay in experimental psychology." In this work, Constantine Constantius tells the story of a love affair. In the original version, the hero commits suicide when his beloved becomes engaged to another. Kierkegaard changed the ending when his real-life love interest, Regine, became engaged to someone else very near the publication of this work. In the new version, the lover expresses delight at his freedom (see Chapter 1 for a quotation from this work).

- *Philosophical Fragments* discusses the subjective approach to knowledge. To the Greeks, the truth was in man, waiting to be discovered.

Therefore, to know oneself was to find God. In this work, Kierkegaard discusses the paradoxical nature of religion, using Christ as an example of the absolute paradox, because he is God in time. Kierkegaard contradicts the Socratic thinking and offers another, that truth must be brought from an outside source because it is so absurd and that something must change within the seeker—miraculous power of divine grace—in order for him to recognize the truth:

One who gives the learner not only the Truth, but also the condition for understanding it, is more than a teacher . . . ; if it is to be done, it must be done by God himself.

- *The Concept of Dread (Anxiety),* published within days of *Philosophical Fragments,* addresses the dogmatic problem of original sin. Written under the pseudonym Vigilius Haufniensis ("alert or watchful Copenhager"), the work is a psychological essay that describes dread and what causes it. You can read more about this work in Chapter 6.

- *Stages on Life's Way* continues the discussion of the approaches to life first introduced in *Either/Or.* This work was put together by the fictional editor Hilarious Bookbinder from three manuscripts left to him. The first part is modeled on Plato's *Symposium* and describes a banquet attended by five aesthetics who seek truth in wine. The second part is a moral treatise, "Some Reflections on Marriage in Answer to Objections," written by the Judge. The third is a journal describing the love affair of Quidam (male) and Quaedam (female). The story of the two lovers is similar to Kierkegaard's courtship of Regine. Quidam is passionate about spirituality and tries to convince Quaedam, who does not share his religious passion, to get involved in his spiritual quests. Quidam proposes to Quaedam and then seeks to break the engagement. He then questions whether God has put him in the situation for a purpose: redemption. Kierkegaard explores the theme of sacrifice here.

- *The Concluding Unscientific Postscript* continues the discussion of faith from earlier works. In this work, Kierkegaard presents the idea that faith is a constant act, a continual striving. He purports that, when one claims to have knowledge of a thing, one does so solely through an act of faith. You can read more about this work in Chapter 7.

- *The Sickness Unto Death* depicts sin as a sickness in a person's self; sin is the opposite of faith. Kierkegaard offers that the sickness does not have to be unto death if the patient recognizes his condition and discovers the way to healing.

- *Works of Love,* one of the works published under Kierkegaard's name, provides a description of different kinds of love, with Christian love representing perfection. Kierkegaard maintained that it was our duty to love God and our neighbor:

The Christian teaching is to love the neighbor, to love the whole race, all men, even one's enemy, and to make no exception, either of partiality or of dislike. There is only One whom a man may with the truth of the eternal love better than himself, that is God.

- *Training in Christianity* was Kierkegaard's favorite work. In it, he attempts to define "what it means to be a Christian—in Christendom." Kierkegaard's answer to that is to be "just as contemporary with His presence on earth as were those [first] contemporaries." Opening with and citing throughout the first part, the Bible passage "Come hither, all ye that labor and are heavy laden, I will give you rest," the work asks and answers questions such as, "Can one learn from history anything about Christ?" and "Can one prove from history that Christ was God?" (Kierkegaard's answer to both: no.)

Kierkegaard's Philosophy Continues

Kierkegaard's work was not wildly popular during his lifetime. It was discovered after his death and championed by Danish critic Georg Brandes. Kierkegaard's work became widely read and discussed in Germany and France, and then in the United States. He had immediate influence on Heidegger's *Being and Time,* although his influence is not acknowledged by Heidegger. His viewpoints were also read and explored by Scandinavians Henrik Ibsen and August Strindberg. These two, with Nietzsche, became central icons for the modernism movement in Berlin.

Existential themes introduced by Kierkegaard are still relevant today. Other famous existentialists include Sartre and Camus.

Either/Or

> *Most men pursue pleasure with such breathless haste that they hurry past it.*
> —Søren Kierkegaard

Either/Or was Kierkegaard's first major work. It was written after his broken engagement with Regine and after the publication and acceptance of his dissertation (a work that discussed Socrates's use of irony). In *Either/Or*, Kierkegaard presents two approaches to life: the aesthetical and the ethical. Instead of telling readers what is right and wrong, in *Either/Or* Kierkegaard creates a unique collection of pieces that leave the reader to figure out for himself which approach is best.

This chapter explains how *Either/Or* is organized and who its "authors" are. The chapter also provides a look at the key themes presented in this work.

The "Authors" of Either/Or

Either/Or is a collection of material put together by the fictitious editor, Victor Emerita ("the victorious hermit"). At the start of the work, Victor tells how he came to find and publish it: He had been pondering philosophical issues and happened upon a work that perfectly illustrated his themes.

Either/Or is comprised of several papers, supposedly written by different authors—referred to as Author A, Johannes, and Author B (or the Judge).

Author A

Author A presents the aesthetic view of life, a life based on the pursuit of pleasure and the avoidance of boredom. The parts written by Author A provide various levels of this lifestyle, revealed through the actions and thoughts of the characters in various situations. Through these characters, Kierkegaard provides a hierarchy of the aesthetic, from the lowest type (the person unaware even of his choices) to the highest (the man who has realized the emptiness of a purely aesthetic life but sticks with it because he is afraid).

Johannes

In addition, Author A includes *The Diary of the Seducer,* a work Author A claims not to have written. Instead, Author A claims he has copied the diary of a friend, Johannes. This work is told from the viewpoint of Johannes and describes, from his narration and letters, the seduction of Cordelia.

Author B or the Judge

The second part of *Either/Or* is written by Author B, Judge Wilhelm. The Judge lives an orderly, ethical life, with faith in God and society. In his letters to Author A, he urges Author A to reconsider his life and see the mistake in his choices. He urges Author A to see that Author A is at the mercy of his circumstances and, thus, view the isolation and gloominess of the aesthetic approach. He advocates that Author A consider a different approach, an ethical approach, to life.

How Either/Or Is Set Up

Reading Kierkegaard can be somewhat like opening a Russian nesting doll, in which one doll is inside another, which is inside another, and so on. In *Either/Or,* there is a made-up editor, Victor Emerita, who publishes the papers of Author A, who includes in his papers a transcription of a diary that is opened with a preface by another person who says he found the diary in a friend's desk. To make things even more complicated, at the end of the work, the editor says that, even though he has divided the work into papers from Author A and from Author B, he thinks they may both be the same person!

In *Either/Or,* Kierkegaard invites his readers to participate in the story and then draw their own conclusions. This means of indirect communication, Kierkegaard thought, was the only true way of relating subjective truth. When reading *Either/Or,* it helps to understand how the work is organized and which of the "authors" is presenting each view.

Knowing the various parts of *Either/Or* is important, because it provides you a better understanding of just what part of the work you're reading, from whose viewpoint the material is presented, and how it relates to the other parts.

The following pieces make up the papers of Author A:

- "Diapsalmata," a collection of short anecdotes and observations such as the following:

What is a poet? An unhappy person who conceals profound anguish in his heart but whose lips are so formed that as sighs and cries pass over them they sound like beautiful music.

- "The Immediate Stages of the Erotic, or the Musical Erotic," an essay about music and religion.

- "The Ancient Tragical Motif as Reflected in the Modern," an essay that discusses ancient and modern tragedies. This essay as well as the next two were intended to be read to a "fellowship of the dead" (Symparanekromenoi) club.

- "Shadowgraphs: A Psychological Pastime," a lecture, intended to be read to the club, which talks about modern heroines.

- "The Unhappiest One," a lecture about who has the right to be called the unhappiest one.

- "The First Love," an essay of praise for a comedy.

- "Crop Rotation: An Attempt at a Theory of Social Prudence," a discussion of how to avoid boredom. You'll often find this piece (or a section of it) in anthologies of Kierkegaard's writings.

- "The Diary of a Seducer," the story of Johannes and his courtship of Cordelia. This is another piece often included in anthologies. It has many similarities to Kierkegaard's own courtship of Regine.

In addition to the preceding papers, the editor also publishes several letters written by Author B to Author A. These include the following:

- "The Aesthetic Validity of Marriage," a pious defense of marriage.

- "Equilibrium between the Aesthetic and the Ethical in the Development of Personality," a letter that discusses the importance of life choices.

■ "Ultimatum," a letter that includes a transcription of a sermon. The sermon's main message is that, in relation to God, we are always in the wrong.

Life from an Aesthetic View

The goal of the aesthetic, according to Kierkegaard, is to manipulate the people and events around him so that they are entertaining. The aesthetic is a voyeur. The various aesthetic viewpoints presented in the writings of Author A provide a sense of what Kierkegaard proposed are important to the aesthetic (and what the aesthetic's flaws are).

When reading the first part of *Either/Or* and considering the values, actions, and morals of the aesthetic lifestyle, note Kierkegaard's use of irony. When he presents these views, he is doing so ironically so that the reader draws his or her own conclusions about the life and views of this particular author. Also, remember Kierkegaard's courtship of Regine. They met when Regine was 14 (too young for courtship) and Kierkegaard was 21, similar to the characters in the diary. Kierkegaard draws from his own experience, although it is clear he did love Regine. That is, he did not pursue her in the way presented in *Either/Or*.

A Fear of Commitment

The section of observations and anecdotes ("Diapsalmata") illustrates the lack of commitment or involvement in the aesthetic's own life and choices. The following excerpt from Author A's writings in *Either/Or* makes the point:

> I do not care for anything. I do not care to ride, for the exercise is too violent. I do not care to walk, walking is too strenuous. I do not care to lie down, for I should either have to remain lying, and I do not care to do that, or I should have to get up again, and I do not care to do that either. Summa summarum: I do not care at all.

The aesthetic lives for possibility (what might be) rather than actuality (what is):

> If I were to wish for anything, I should not wish for wealth and power, but for the passionate sense of the potential, for the eye which, ever young and ardent, sees the possible. Pleasure disappoints, possibility

never. And what wine is so sparkling, what so fragrant, what so intoxicating, as possibility!

Boredom Is the Root of Evil

In the section called "Crop Rotation: An Attempt at a Theory of Social Prudence," Author A, an aesthetic, says that "boredom is the root of evil." He traces the start and consequences of boredom:

> The history of this [boredom] can be traced from the very beginning of the world. The gods were bored, and so they created man. Adam was bored because he was alone, and so Eve was created. Thus boredom entered the world, and increased in proportion to the increase of population. Adam was bored alone; then Adam and Eve were bored together; then Adam and Eve and Cain and Abel were bored *en famille;* then the population of the world increased, and the peoples were bored *en masse.* To divert themselves they conceived the idea of constructing a tower high enough to reach the heavens. The idea is itself as boring as the tower was high, and constitutes a terrible proof of how boredom gained the upper hand. The nations were scattered over the earth, just as people now travel abroad, but they continued to be bored.

This piece goes on to provide some advice on how to overcome boredom and uses the analogy (from the essay title) of crop rotation. He advises things like limiting yourself so that you become fertile in imagination, giving up hope ("one should never permit hope to be taken aboard one's own ship, least of all as pilot; for hope is a faithless shipmaster"), practicing forgetting ("Forgetting is the shears with which you cut away what you cannot use, doing it under the supreme direction of memory"), guarding against friendship ("The art of remembering and forgetting will also insure against sticking fast in some relationship to life, and make possible the realization of complete freedom"), avoiding marriage ("When two beings fall in love with one another and begin to suspect that they were made for each other, it is time to have the courage to break it off; for by going on they have everything to lose and nothing to gain"), and avoiding business.

The Tale of Seduction

The narrative account of the seduction also provides a glimpse into the values and actions of the aesthetic. In this story, the narrator Johannes plots the seduction of Cordelia, from spotting her to the first smile to the engagement. To the seducer, the main goal isn't the girl, but the act of seduction or the thrill of the chase:

> No, when one can so arrange it that a girl's only desire is to give herself freely, when she feels that her whole happiness depends on this, when she almost begs to make this free submission, then there is first true enjoyment.

Johannes pursues Cordelia relentlessly (all the while knowing that he doesn't really want her in the end). He writes:

> And when I have gazed and gazed again, considered and again considered this multitudinous variety, when I have smiled, sighed, flattered, threatened, desired, tempted, laughed, wept, hoped, feared, won, lost— then I shut up my fan, and gather the fragments into a unity, the parts into a whole. Then my soul is glad, my heart beats, my passion is aflame. This one woman, the only woman in all the world, she must belong to me, she must be mine.

In the end, he breaks the engagement and writes, "[I]t is over now, and I hope never to see her again. . . . I will have no farewell with her; nothing is more disgusting to me than a woman's tears and a woman's prayers."

Moving to an Ethical View

The second part of *Either/Or* is composed by Author B, or Judge Wilhem. The Judge presents a contrasting view of life and, in his letters, urges Author A to reconsider his life, despair, and change. He does so by pointing out the flaws in Author A's aesthetic lifestyle:

> This is what is sad when one contemplates human life, that so many live out their lives in quiet lostness . . . they live, as it were, away from themselves and vanish like shadows. Their immortal souls are blown away, and they are not disquieted by the question of its immortality, because they are already disintegrated before they die.

He points out the constant striving in the life of the aesthetic:

> There are people so weak that they need loud noise and a distracting environment in order to be able to work. Why is this, unless for the fact that they have no command over themselves, except in the inverse sense. . . . It is for this reason you are afraid of peace and quietness and

repose. You are within yourself only when there is opposition, but therefore you are never within yourself.

The Judge indicts Author A's lack of involvement in his own life and any relationships and what he loses by this approach. He writes, "Your occupation consists in preserving your hiding place, and that you succeed in doing, for your mask is the most enigmatical of all. In fact you are nothing; you are merely a relation to others." He challenges Author A:

Do you not know that there comes a midnight hour when every one has to throw off his mask? Do you believe that life will always let itself be mocked? Do you think you can slip away a little before midnight in order to avoid this? Or are you not terrified of it?

The Judge sums up what is missing with this attitude when he states, "[H]e who cannot reveal himself cannot love, and he who cannot love is the most unhappy man of all."

After all the predictions and cajoling, the Judge reminds Author A that it is possible to change. He writes, "[Y]ou can win what is the chief thing in life—win yourself, acquire your own self."

An Ethical Approach to Life

After urging Author A to reconsider his (lack of) choice and his devil-may-care approach to life, the Judge presents what he considers the proper approach to life. The Judge does not deny the pleasures of the aesthetic life. Instead, he thinks it is possible to synthesize the two into a balanced life. This approach is discussed in "Equilibrium between the Aesthetic and the Ethical in the Development of Personality." He states

. . . men are divided into two great classes: those who predominantly live in hope, and those who predominantly live in recollection. Both have a wrong relation to time. The healthy individual lives at once both in hope and recollection.

The Judge discusses the aesthetic and ethical approaches and summarizes them in this passage (also referencing the title of the work and its meaning):

My either/or does not in the first instance denote the choice between good and evil, it denotes the choice whereby one chooses good *and* evil/or excludes them. . . . That the man who chooses good and evil chooses the good is indeed true, but this becomes evident only afterwards; for the aesthetical is not the evil but neutrality, and that is the reason why I affirmed that it is the ethical which constitutes the choice. . . . It is, therefore, not so much a question of choosing between willing the good *or* the evil, as of choosing to *will.*

The Judge's part of the work also includes the letter, "The Aesthetic Validity of Marriage." In this, he discusses love, how romantic love is "built upon an illusion," and how conjugal love is preferred. He describes this type of love as "faithful, constant, humble, patient, long-suffering, indulgent, sincere, contented, vigilant, willing, joyful."

The Judge also presents the various approaches to life again stating:

If you cannot reach the point of seeing the aesthetical, the ethical, and the religious as three great allies, if you do not know how to conserve the unity of the diverse appearances which everything assumes in these diverse spheres, then life is devoid of meaning, then one must grant that you are justified in maintaining your pet theory that one can say of everything, "Do it or don't do it—you will regret both."

A Summary of Themes from Either/Or

From this first work of Kierkegaard's, you can see the emergence of some of his key themes. First is the directive to make a choice. The Judge describes the evolution of choice through life:

I think of my early youth, when without clearly comprehending what it is to make a choice I listened with childish trust to the talk of my elders, and the instant of choice was solemn and venerable, although in choosing I was only following the instructions of another person. I think of the occasions in my later life when I stood at the crossways, when my soul was matured in the hour of decision. I think of the many occasions in life less important but by no means indifferent to me, when it was a question of making a choice. For although there is only one situation in which either/or has absolute significance, namely when truth, righteousness, and holiness are lined up on one side, and lust and base propensities and obscure passions and perdition on the other; yet it is always important to choose rightly.

Second is his admonition to choose correctly. In Kierkegaard's view, the aesthetic life is void of meaning but the aesthetic can despair and make a choice, choosing instead an ethical approach to life.

Choosing correctly doesn't mean following advice blindly or accepting this view without consideration. Choosing correctly involves inner reflection and personal responsibility.

Either/Or illustrates the emergence of an existential viewpoint where choice and individual responsibility are key. Kierkegaard presents individuals that are confronted with a choice and through their stories the reader sees how the actions and choices define (or do not define) a person.

Kierkegaard also touches on the theme of sacrifice, especially in discussing cases where marriage may not be appropriate for a person (as in his own case). He continues this theme in one of his next works, *Fear and Trembling*, the topic of the next chapter.

4 Fear and Trembling

Faith is a miracle, and yet no man is excluded from it; for that in which all human life is unified is passion, and faith is a passion.

—Søren Kierkegaard

Fear and Trembling continues Kierkegaard's quest after questions of religion. In particular, Kierkegaard gives the reader a definition of faith in this work. He does so by discussing the Bible story of Abraham and Isaac. Like *Either/Or*, *Fear and Trembling* was published under a pseudonym and includes different elements.

This chapter starts by describing the parts that make up *Fear and Trembling* and then discusses its relevant themes.

Abraham, the Father of Faith

Abraham was known as the Father of Faith, and Kierkegaard turns to the most well-known story about Abraham for answers about faith. Abraham was childless until he was 86. Then (with the consent of his wife, Sarah) he fathered a son, Ishmael, with an Egyptian maid named Hagar. When Abraham was 99, God spoke to him and told him that Sarah would bear him a son and that Abraham would become the "father of many nations" (Genesis 17:4). When Abraham heard this message, he laughed. He was 99 after all, and Sarah was 90. When he told Sarah, she also laughed. This angered God who said, "Is anything too hard for the Lord?" (Genesis 18:14). They did have a son, named Isaac.

God tested Abraham's faith, and it is this test of faith that Kierkegaard elaborated on in *Fear and Trembling*:

And it came to pass after these things, that God did tempt Abraham, and said unto him, Abraham: and he said, Behold here I am. And he said, Take now thy son, thine only son Isaac, whom thou lovest, and get thee into the land of Moriah; and offer him there for a burnt offering upon one of the mountains which I will tell thee of.

Abraham and Isaac traveled to Moriah and collected wood for the altar. Isaac asked his father, "Behold the fire and the wood: but where is the lamb for a burnt offering?" Abraham answered, "My son, God will provide himself a lamb for a burnt offering" (Genesis 22:7).

They arrived at the place God selected and Abraham bound his son and laid him on the altar. He took his knife and prepared to slay his son, but he was stopped by God: "Lay not thine hand upon the lad, neither do thou any thing unto him: for now I know that thou fearest God, seeing thou hast not withheld thy son, thine only son from me" (Genesis 22:12).

Kierkegaard maintained that most Christians didn't think deeply about this story, but hurried through it to the end, where Isaac was saved. He didn't think they fully understood the story—or wanted to, given its difficult message. He writes in *Fear and Trembling,* "[O]ne wants nothing of the fear, the distress, the paradox. One flirts with the outcome aesthetically; it comes as unexpectedly and yet as effortlessly as a prize in the lottery; and having heard the outcome one is improved."

In *Fear and Trembling,* Kierkegaard challenges the reader to more closely examine this store, and Kierkegaard wonders how this action is judged ethically. Like his other writing, he does not present his ideas directly to the reader but does so indirectly through stories and pieces written and collected by the "author" of the work, Johannes de Silentio ("John the Silent").

The Parts of Fear and Trembling

If you read all of *Fear and Trembling,* you can get a sense of the different pieces that make up the work. But if you read part of the work from an anthology, knowing which part you're reading and how it fits into the overall structure is important. *Fear and Trembling* is comprised of these parts:

- **"Preface"** sets the opening for the story to follow and introduces the author, who claims, "The present author is no philosopher, he has not understood the System, nor does he know if there really is one, or if it has been completed."

- **"Attunement"** consists of different imagined versions of Abraham and Isaac's trip to Moriah. The author creates four scenarios of the trip and its outcome.

- **"Speech in Praise of Abraham"** discusses the need for heroes and poets to sing the praises of these heroes.

- **"Problemata,"** the second half of the book, starts with a Preamble and includes a discussion and comparison of the "knights of infinite resignation" and the "knights of faith." The rest of this section includes three "problems." The first asks whether there can be "a teleological suspension of the ethical." The second asks whether there is "an absolute duty to God." The final section, "Was It Ethically Defensible of Abraham to Conceal His Purpose from Sarah, from Eleazar, from Isaac," discusses whether Abraham should have told Sarah about the trip.

- **"Epilogue,"** the final part, discusses faith as being the ultimate passion and ridicules those inclined to go beyond faith.

The following sections discuss the different parts and their contents in more detail.

The Preface: Setting the Scene

The purpose of the Preface is to set up the following parts, giving readers clues about the author and his purpose. The author claims to be "no philosopher." He also mentions "the System," a reference to Hegel. Hegel, the most dominant philosopher when Kierkegaard was writing, created an entire system of thought. (You can read more about Hegel in Chapter 2.) Hegel believed knowledge was objective and that his system of thought was all encompassing.

Hegel was influenced by Descartes, and he is also referenced in the Preface to *Fear and Trembling*. One of the quests of philosophy was to describe all knowledge. Descartes (who said, "I think therefore I am"), as a rationalist, set out to prove that, through rational thought, the human mind was sufficient to gain knowledge of the central issues confronting humanity, thus rejecting the church's claim that any knowledge of such matters was gained only through the church. Because math followed a set of reasons and could be proved deductively (from the specific to the general), he thought the same method used for math could be used on other topics. Philosophy studies would place him in the branch of philosophy called *epistemology.* This branch is concerned with determining what constitutes knowledge and asks questions like what are the ways to knowledge, and how can we justify confidence or belief in the certainty of our knowledge. In *The Story of Philosophy,* Bryan McGee sums up Descartes this way:

> Descartes was a key figure in persuading people in the West that certainty was available in our knowledge of the world. To obtain it you needed to follow the right method, but if you did that you could build up an impregnable science that would give you rock-hard reliable knowledge.

Kierkegaard clearly does not hold the same views as Descartes. He pokes fun at this type of thinking: "As far as his own weak head is concerned, the thought of what huge heads everyone must have in order to have such huge thoughts is already enough" *(Fear and Trembling).* He talks about living "in an age where passion has been done away with for the sake of science" and concludes, "I prostrate myself before any systematic bag-searcher: this is not the System." In jest he wishes "all good on the System and on the Danish shareholders in that omnibus, for it will hardly become a tower." The last remark is a reference to a Bible passage from Luke:

> For which of you, intending to build a tower, sitteth not down first, and counteth the cost, whether he have sufficient to finish it? Lest haply, after he hath laid the foundation, and is not able to finish it, all that beheld it begin to mock him, saying, This man began to build, and was not able to finish. (Luke 14)

The Preface, then, outlines the author's thoughts on the current thinking of the time (Hegel's System). This sets up the background for the new ideas this nonsystematic author has and presents in the rest of the work.

Attunement: What Happened on that Fateful Trip to Moriah?

In the Attunement, the author tells the story of a man who ponders the story of Abraham and Isaac and who has "one wish, actually to see Abraham, and one longing, to have been witness to those events" *(Fear and Trembling).* To that effect, the author imagines four different scenarios:

- In the first version, Abraham told Isaac what was to happen, but when Isaac "clung to Abraham's knees, pleaded at his feet, begged for his young life," Abraham did not relent. Instead of telling Isaac why (that it is God's will), Abraham pretends he wants to kill Isaac because it is "better that he believe I am a monster than he lose faith in Thee."

- In the second version, Abraham goes to the mountain, kills a ram, and returns home. Because he "could not forget that God had demanded this of him," Abraham's "eye was darkened, he saw joy no more."

- In the third version, Abraham goes alone to Moriah and begs God "to forgive his sin at having been willing to sacrifice Isaac." Again, Abraham has no peace or understanding: "He could not comprehend that it was a sin to have been willing to sacrifice to God the best he owned."

- In the fourth version, Abraham takes Isaac to the mountain and starts to sacrifice him but stops. In this version, Isaac sees the knife and loses his faith.

All these scenarios are presented to get the reader to really participate, to imagine, to *think* about the story instead of just reading through it. This practice of immersing the reader in a setting and getting the reader to participate in the process rather than just accepting answers was originally developed by Plato. In doing so, Kierkegaard wants the reader to see that there is no easy answer. The storyteller in the end collapses and says, "Yet no one was as great as Abraham; who is able to understand him?"

Now the problem is defined, and as a reader, you can see that it's not a simple one. Kierkegaard next presents the issues in Problemata, starting with the Preamble.

The Preamble: Knight versus Knight

The opening of the Preamble is summed up in *The Kierkegaard Reader:*

> The Preamble . . . takes issue with people who are content with the "large truths" of "conventional wisdom." . . . They probably know the story of Abraham by heart, but never lose sleep over it: they are serenely untroubled by the fact that if anyone else behaved like Abraham, it would be "a sin, a crying sin."

This section goes on to imagine two contrasting knights: the knight of infinite resignation and the knight of faith. The knight of infinite resignation is the one who doesn't believe that all is possible with God. He is infinitely resigned. He thinks "in the world of the finite . . . this was and remained an impossibility."

Contrast this to the knight of faith: "This [the impossibility] is quite clear to the knight of the faith, so the only thing that can save him is the absurd, and this he grasps by faith. So he recognizes the impossibility, and that very instant believes in the absurd." Kierkegaard goes on to describe the knight of faith. He does not stand out in a crowd. There is "nothing of that aloof and superior nature whereby one recognizes the knight of the infinite. . . . If one did not know him, it would be impossible to distinguish him from the rest."

The Preamble explains Kierkegaard's concept of the double movement; the knight of the faith, when "he resigned everything infinitely," then "grasped everything again by virtue of the absurd." In Kierkegaard's work, this double movement consists of the movement of the infinite resignation and the movement of faith. The story of Abraham illustrates just that concept for, "By faith Abraham did not renounce his claim upon Isaac, but by faith he got Isaac back." By believing in this paradox—that he gains Isaac by giving him up—Abraham becomes the father of faith.

Problem 1: Can God Trump Ethics?

Next Kierkegaard wonders how Abraham's actions are viewed ethically in the problem entitled "Is There Such a Thing as a Teleological Suspension of the Ethical?" (*Teleological* means relating to teleology, the study of ends or goals. Macgee, in *The Story of Philosophy,* defines a teleological explanation as "one that explains something in terms of the ends it serves.")

Kierkegaard questions the ethics of Abraham's actions by contrasting them with those of the tragic hero, focusing in particular on the story of Agamemnon. King Agamemnon offended a Greek god and, in order to set sail and save his country during the Trojan War, he was required to sacrifice his daughter Iphigenia. His sacrifice is known to others and is praised: "[S]oon the whole nation will be cognizant of his pain, but also cognizant of his exploit, that for the welfare of the whole he was willing to sacrifice her" (*Fear and Trembling*). Kierkegaard concludes "the tragic hero still remains within the ethical."

Kierkegaard contrasts Agamemnon's sacrifice with Abraham's: "With Abraham the situation was different. By his act he overstepped the ethical entirely and possessed a higher telos outside of it." His actions were "not for the sake of saving a people, not to maintain the idea of the state." Kierkegaard points out that Abraham's is a personal choice: "[W]hereas the tragic hero is great by reason of his moral virtue, Abraham is great by reason of a personal virtue."

Abraham cannot tell anyone of his ordeal. He cannot justify himself saying, "The future will show I was right." Yet if his actions are wrong, Kierkegaard concludes, then he is a murderer. And if he's right, then there are instances in which one can suspend the ethical for a higher purpose.

Kierkegaard shows a similar connection with the story of Mary and concludes of both:

> She needs no wordly admiration, as little as Abraham needs our tears, for she was no heroine and he no hero, but both of them became greater than that, not by means of being relieved of the distress, the agony, and the paradox, but because of these.

Again, this is the paradox Kierkegaard called "virtue of the absurd"— the paradoxical notion that only the absurd is a "reasonable" choice, since reason must be suspended and subjective passion embraced. In addition to this example, Kierkegaard discusses this concept in many of his other works.

Problem 2: Do We Have an Absolute Duty to God?

The second section (or problem) is summed up in *The Kierkegaard Reader:*

> The second *problema* asks whether there is "an absolute duty to God" and contrasts the lonely figure of Abraham—the "knight of faith" who has to violate ethical norms out of his individual duty to God—with that of a "tragic hero" whose beautiful soul is comfortably at home with the rest of the ethical community.

Again, Abraham is not a tragic hero; he is much more than that. The tragic hero is eventually understood and his sacrifice is noted. He is not only part of the community, but a hero to them, someone who is admired and respected all the more because of his actions. Abraham's relationship was with God alone; he could not seek outside support for his actions. He could not find a reasonable or sympathetic explanation, nor did he want to. He held fast to his duty to God, even if that meant being misunderstood and shunned.

Problem 3: Should Abraham Have Told?

The final problem looks into whether Abraham should have told his wife, Sarah, and his son Isaac about the sacrifice, and again compares these actions with that of classical tragedy.

Kierkegaard presents the view that concealment and then recognition of the "resolving factor" (why the hero acts as he does) are essential parts of tragic drama. He refers again to the drama of Agamemnon. The tragic hero and his actions are in line with ethics, and the reader can relate: "The tragic hero, the darling of ethics, is a purely human being, and he is someone I can understand, someone whose every undertaking is out in the open" *(Fear and Trembling)*.

He contrasts the typical tragic hero with the role of Abraham, who does not speak and explain his actions. Kierkegaard maintains that, even if Abraham wanted to speak, he could not because his actions are not understandable. He writes "Abraham is silent—but he *cannot* speak, therein lies the distress and anguish. For if when I speak I cannot make myself understood, I do not speak even if I keep talking without stop day and night."

Kierkegaard underlies again the paradox of the actions and shows the reader that faith requires the acceptance of such paradoxes. He summarizes again the double movement Abraham makes:

> He makes the infinite movement of resignation and gives up his claim to Isaac, something no one can understand because it is a private undertaking. But then he further makes, and at every moment is making, the movement of faith. This is his comfort. For he says, "Nevertheless it won't happen, or if it does the Lord will give me a new Isaac on the strength of the absurd."

The Kierkegaard Reader sums up the paradox in this way:

> [Abraham] is not the hero whose tragic destiny is eventually made clear. . . . He is a paradox, and can be understood only in the way that paradoxes are understood: not by being resolved, but by having their unintelligibility properly acknowledged.

The reader should just accept that he or she won't fully understand these actions. That is, faith cannot be mediated.

The Epilogue

The Epilogue concludes with Kierkegaard making fun of people who want to go further than faith. To him, faith is both the end ("Faith is the highest passion in a human being.") and the continuing challenge for all ("So long as the generation only worries about its task, which is the highest it can attain to, it cannot grow weary. The task is always enough for a human lifetime.").

Major Themes in Fear and Trembling

Fear and Trembling was one of Kierkegaard's favorite works. In his journal, he wrote, "Oh, when I am dead—then *Fear and Trembling* will alone give me the name of an immortal author. Then it will be read, then too it will be translated into foreign tongues; and people will almost shudder at the frightful pathos of the book." Many of Kierkegaard's key themes are illustrated in this book.

For example, Kierkegaard struggles with his own choices, in particular, his sacrifice of Regine, in this passage:

He [the knight] has comprehended the deep secret that even in loving another person one must be sufficient unto oneself. He no longer takes a finite interest in what the princess is doing, and precisely this is proof that he has made the movement infinitely. Here one may have an opportunity to see whether the movement on the part of a particular person is true or fictitious. There was one who also believed that he had made the movement; but lo, time passed, the princess did something else, she married—a prince, let us say; then his soul lost the elasticity of resignation. Thereby he knew that he had not made the movement rightly.

Regine did marry at the time of this work, and Kierkegaard continued to question his decision.

Another relevant theme to Kierkegaard's lifetime is Kierkegaard's reaction and response to the predominant philosopher at the time (Hegel). Hegel's System stressed the importance of the individual within the whole of society, but Kierkegaard disagreed, emphasizing the individual and the individual's choice. The underlying existential concept of choice is illustrated in this passage from *Fear and Trembling:*

> The infinite resignation is the shirt that we read about in the old fable. The thread is spun of tears, the cloth bleached with tears, the shirt sewn with tears. . . . The imperfection in the fable is that a third party can manufacture this shirt. The secret in life is that everyone must sew it for himself.

Kierkegaard believed that faith was an issue for the individual and that, in sorting out the issue, the individual cannot rely on doctrine or advice from others. He has to make the choice alone:

> When a person sets out on the tragic hero's admittedly hard path there are many who lend him advice; but he who walks the narrow path of faith no one can advise, no one understand.

In Kierkegaard's view, the end result is the individual before God (as contrasted with existentialists who didn't believe in God). At the end of Problemata 3, he concludes

> But none can understand Abraham. And yet think what he achieved! To remain true to his love. But he who loves God has no need of tears, needs no admiration, and forgets his suffering in love, indeed forgets so completely that afterwards not the least hint of his pain would remain were God himself not to remember it; for God sees in secret and knows the distress and counts the tears and forgets nothing.

Kierkegaard's next work combines the themes from *Fear and Trembling* (faith as a paradox) and *Repetition* (recollection and repetition). The next chapter discusses this work, entitled *Philosophical Fragments.*

5 Philosophical Fragments

Once man understood little, but that little moved him profoundly. Now he understands much, but it does not move him, or it moves him only superficially, like a grimace.

—Søren Kierkegaard

In *Philosophical Fragments*, Kierkegaard continues the theme of understanding faith. In this work, Kierkegaard questions how we come to know something (in particular, how we come to know religious truth). This work, like Kierkegaard's previous works, was published under a pseudonym and was a reaction to current philosophical thought at the time, in particular Hegel but also others.

This chapter provides background information so that you can see what Kierkegaard was responding to and influenced by. The chapter also discusses the way Kierkegaard presents his point of view about matters of faith and religious truth.

The Philosophy of the Time: Hegel and Lessing

One challenge in reading a philosopher so many years after his death is that you often have to understand not only what his contemporaries were writing about, but also many of his predecessors. Kierkegaard is no different in this regard; an understanding of those who influenced him will provide a better understanding of *Philosophical Fragments*.

Hegel Again

Kierkegaard was clearly reacting to Hegel in his writing, but modern readers don't easily pick up the nuances and clues indicating this connection. Hegel has largely disappeared as an important philosopher unless one is studying nineteenth-century philosophy, but Kierkegaard, who wasn't widely read during the nineteenth century and early twentieth century, is still more widely read today.

The title *Philosophical Fragments,* for instance, is a rebuke of Hegel's work. Hegel thought his System was all-encompassing and that he had, once and for all, solved all philosophical problems. Although he acknowledged that a few issues may need to be addressed in the future, Hegel believed that they could be handled easily in a short postscript by his disciples. Kierkegaard's book title, then, pokes fun at Hegel's egotism and overconfidence in his System.

Kierkegaard also wrote a follow-up to *Philosophical Fragments,* a book that is four times as long as *Philosophical Fragments* and is titled *Concluding Unscientific Postscript.* (You can read more about Kierkegaard and his criticism of Hegel in Chapter 7.)

Lessing and the Leap

In addition to Hegel, Kierkegaard was also reacting to the writing of another philosopher, G. E. Lessing (1729–1781). Lessing wrote about what historical proof of the existence of Jesus meant to religious belief. That is, if you proved historically that Jesus lived, did that mean that you must also believe that he was the Son of God? Lessing writes

> If on historical grounds I have no objection to the statement that Christ raised to life a dead man; must I therefore accept it as true that God has a Son who is of the same essence of himself? What is the connection between my inability to raise any significant objection to the evidence of the former and my obligation to believe something against which my reason rebels? *(Lessing's Theological Writings)*

Lessing points out the gap between believing that Christ was risen from the dead and that Christ was the Son of God and of the same essence of God and the necessity to make a leap when he says there is "an ugly broad ditch which I cannot get across, however often and however earnestly I have tried to make the leap."

Kierkegaard agrees with Lessing that there is that gap and continues to ponder the gap and what it meant to religious truth; Kierkegaard believes that reason is useless for many matters, including understanding Christianity. Faith isn't based on reason but just because it isn't based on reason doesn't mean it isn't true. He asserts that proving events historically does not add to the argument. Therefore, Kierkegaard says that you have two options: finding some compromised set of beliefs that conform to rational thought or making the leap. Kierkegaard uses the phrase "virtue of the absurd" to indicate that only what reason says is absurd makes any rational sense when addressing some issues. It is no irony that a "Leap of Faith" is required to cross that gap. *Philosophical Fragments* presents these choices and their implications.

The Author, Johannes Climacus

Now that you know the context of Kierkegaard's writing, you can add one other element of the back story: the pseudonym Kierkegaard uses. Like his use of pseudonyms in his other works, Kierkegaard chose a name that has significance.

Johannes Climacus was a Greek monk, abbot of a church on Mt. Sinai, and author of the work *Klimax tou Paradeisou,* or *Ladder of Paradise.* The book provides a plan for those considering the contemplative life. According to Climacus, first you must fight and subdue your passions. Then you start your ascent of the ladder, which consists of thirty steps and leads you to peace of mind. (This book is still read in Eastern and Orthodox religions.)

D. Anthony Storm, at his Web site, "D. Anthony Storm's Commentary on Kierkegaard" (www.sorenkierkegaard.org/kw7a.htm), describes the purpose of this pseudonym:

> For Kierkegaard, the pseudonym Johannes Climacus represents the subjective approach to knowledge. . . . This ladder is not then the ascent to God but is meant to call to mind an ascending series of logical plateaus, where the logician, represented particularly by Descartes and Hegel, proceeds from one premise to the next. Johannes rejects this method in spiritual matters, thinking it ridiculous to approach the Absolute in any way except through faith. He is concerned with subjective knowledge and with the leap.

Johannes is the guide in *Philosophical Fragments*. Kierkegaard also uses this same pseudonym in the companion work, *Concluding Unscientific Postscript*.

The Setup

The book title *(Philosophical Fragments)* and pseudonym (Johannes Climacus) reveal much of what Kierkegaard is responding to and his angle in this work. Unlike most of his other works, *Philosophical Fragments* is written in an academic style. This book contains five chapters:

- **"A Project of Thought"** sets up the two opposing opinions for comparison and includes the Socratic view and the religious view.

- **"God as Teacher and Saviour: An Essay of the Imagination"** sets up two paths from the religious view Kierkegaard discusses in "A Project of Thought." In this chapter, Kierkegaard maintains that, in order for the divine teacher to have an impact, the teacher must lift his disciples to his level, or lower himself to their level.

- **"The Absolute Paradox: A Metaphysical Caprice"** hits on another Kierkegaard theme, that of the paradox. In this chapter, Kierkegaard makes an "attempt to discover something that thought cannot think" *(Philosophical Fragments)*.

- **"The Case of the Contemporary Disciple"** asks whether Christ's contemporaries would have had an easier time with their faith.

- **"The Disciple at Second Hand"** jumps ahead in time and asks whether those who have lived long *after* Christ have an easier time with their faith.

In addition to these chapters, *Philosophical Fragments* includes the "Interlude," a piece that discusses the idea of free will, especially as it relates to the idea that God always knows what we are going to choose.

How Can You Learn Truth?

Kierkegaard opens his "Project of Thought" with this question: "How far does the Truth admit of being learned?" He then presents two views, the Socratic and the religious.

The Socratic View

In the Socratic view, the truth resides in each individual and must only be remembered or recollected. Kierkegaard writes, "Thus the Truth is not introduced into the individual from without, but was within him all the time" *(Philosophical Fragments)*. If the truth is God, then it follows that you find God in yourself.

Kierkegaard further describes this view and how it relates to Socrates himself:

> In the Socratic view each individual is his own center, and the entire world centers in him, because his self-knowledge is a knowledge of God. It was thus Socrates understood himself, and thus he thought that everyone must understand himself.

Kierkegaard finds a problem with the Socratic view because, in order for this thinking to work, the learner must be in error and must realize on his own that he is in error. Kierkegaard writes, "For what a man knows he cannot seek, since he knows it; and what he does not know he cannot seek, since he does not even know for what to seek."

The Religious View

Kierkegaard presents a viewpoint alternative to the Socratic one—that a teacher is needed. He writes, "Now if the learner is to acquire the Truth, the Teacher must bring it to him; and not only so, but he must also give him the condition necessary for understanding it." He goes on to say that the teacher must transform or remake the learner and, because this can only be done by God, the teacher of Truth must therefore be God:

> But one who gives the learner not only the Truth, but also the condition for understanding it, is more than teacher . . . he would find it necessary not only to transform the learner, but to re-create him from beginning to teach him. But this is something that no human being can do; if it is to be done, it must be done by God himself.

The error or "deprivation," as Kierkegaard calls it, "cannot have been due to an act of God (which would be a contradiction), nor to an accident. . . . [I]t must therefore be due to himself." Kierkegaard calls this error sin.

Now that Kierkegaard has presented God as the teacher, he next imagines God as a teacher and what role God and the learner would have to assume. He presents two options and describes these in Chapter 2 of *Philosophical Fragments.*

God as Teacher

In the second chapter in *Philosophical Fragments,* Kierkegaard uses the analogy of a rich king in love with a humble maiden to illustrate the problem of God the teacher and his humble learners. He sums up the problem in this way:

> . . . the learner is in Error. . . . And yet he is the object of God's love, and God desires to teach him, and is concerned to bring him to equality with himself. If this equality cannot be established, God's love becomes unhappy and his teaching meaningless, since they cannot understand one another.

Kierkegaard then presents the two options: option A, elevating the learner, or option B, the teacher's descent. Option A won't work because God would have to show himself to the learner and then God would be glorified rather than the learner. If the learner is to accept the truth as his own, he cannot do so out of fear, reverence, or awe. Kierkegaard describes option B, where God appears as a servant and sums up why only option B works:

> Every other form of revelation would be a deception in the eyes of love; for either the learner would first have to be changed, and the fact concealed from him that this was necessary (but love does not alter the beloved, it alters itself); or there would be permitted to prevail a frivolous ignorance of the fact that the entire relationship was a delusion.

The truth must come from an equal, and Kierkegaard describes the role the teacher, God, must take:

> God must suffer all things, endure all things, make experience of all things. He must suffer hunger in the desert, he must thirst in the time of his agony, he must be forsaken in death, absolutely like the humblest. . . . His suffering is not that of his death, but his entire life is a story of suffering; and it is love that suffers, the love which gives all is itself in want.

Kierkegaard shows the role the teacher plays in Christianity. If you think back to Kierkegaard's upbringing (his father's insistence on belief in a suffering God), you can see why this image appealed to him. Also, remember that Kierkegaard thought that he sacrificed his own happiness so that Regine could be happy. The theme of self-sacrifice is present in Kierkegaard's own life. Beyond the personal, though, you see Kierkegaard's intense feeling for God and why faith is so important. His belief in Christ incarnate leads him to the absolute paradox, the subject of his next chapter.

The Thought You Cannot Think

Kierkegaard argues that you cannot conceive of something that surpasses your intellectual capabilities. If you succeeded in doing so, you would ultimately fail because you would have disproved your original premise—that something exists that is beyond human understanding. But, Kierkegaard insists, God is beyond understanding.

To Kierkegaard, the absolute paradox was Christ incarnate or God in time. When Christ entered the temporal world and took on a finite existence, his actions could not be understood. The believer, according to Kierkegaard, finds "it impossible to conceive it, could not of itself have discovered it, and when it hears it announced will not be able to understand it" *(Philosophical Fragments)*. Kierkegaard then suggests the same point as Lessing: that when faith and reason conflict, one must choose one or the other. Kierkegaard offers that the learner must make a leap of his own will, with help from his teacher. This leap represented to Kierkegaard the moment of faith and was also a paradox, as he outlined in *Philosophical Fragments:*

> But in that case is not Faith as paradoxical as the Paradox? Precisely so; how else could it have the Paradox for its object, and be happy in its relation to the Paradox? Faith is itself a miracle, and all that holds true of the Paradox also holds true of Faith.

Which Generation Has It Easier?

Kierkegaard next tackles the question of how historical accuracy relates to faith. He introduces this problem by wondering whether Christ's disciples had a faith advantage because of their direct knowledge of him. He concludes that "Faith is not a form of knowledge, for either knowledge is of the eternal, and excludes the temporal and historical as irrelevant, or it is merely historical" *(Philosophical Fragments)*. Kierkegaard denies that contemporaries had an advantage. He does so by discussing the nature of the event:

because accepting something so paradoxical will always require accepting the absurd, time nor circumstance do not factor in.

Kierkegaard also asks the same question of those who lived long after Christ—whether they had an advantage, since the message should have been clarified and refined through the years. Kierkegaard concludes that it was just as easy for contemporaries of Christ to make a mistake as those who lived later. He states that what matters in relation to faith "cannot be communicated from one person to another." He again writes that "faith is not a form of knowledge but an act of freedom, an expression of will." Because of its nature as an experience, a choice, later generations face the same issues as those contemporaries of Christ. In *Philosophical Fragments,* Kierkegaard writes

> The faith of later generations is of course grounded in contemporary testimony, but only in the same way as the faith of the contemporaries was grounded in direct cognition and sensation. But that was never the basis of contemporary faith, and later generations cannot base their faith on testimony either.

He cautions the danger of new generations relying on conclusions from previous generations rather than finding out for themselves:

> If each generation wants simply to bequeath a splendid set of conclusions to the next, will not these conclusions become misunderstandings? Is not Venice constructed over the sea? Suppose it became so densely built up that a generation was born that no longer was aware of this fact—would it not be a terrible misunderstanding if the present generation allowed the piles to rot away so that the city sank? Yet conclusions founded on a paradox are humanly speaking built over a yawning chasm, and their total content, which is handed down to individuals only on the express understanding that they are sustained by a paradox, cannot be inherited like a settled estate since their entire value trembles in the balance.

In *Kierkegaard: A Very Short Introduction,* Patrick Gardiner sums up Chapters 4 and 5 of *Philosophical Fragments:*

> Religiously speaking, neither has the edge over the other. In every case faith demands, not just a leap, but a leap into the rationally unthinkable which presupposes divine assistance. . . . Faith, as Kierkegaard understands it, is not a matter of superior evidence or conditions of observation; its possibility depends, as has been seen, on a miracle.

Themes in Philosophical Fragments

Philosophical Fragments continued Kierkegaard's writing about issues of faith and religion, in particular how they relate to knowledge. (He'll continue his discussion from *Philosophical Fragments* in his later work entitled *Concluding Unscientific Postscript,* covered in Chapter 7.) As a reader, you'll note some of the same issues and concepts Kierkegaard has discussed in other works.

Faith, for instance, is still a challenge for Kierkegaard. To him, faith requires a leap from the known to the unknown; it also requires acceptance of the paradoxical nature of religion.

Knowledge is not within man, waiting to be discovered, as Socrates professed. Kierkegaard says it is outside of man and to find real truth requires a teacher and that teacher can only be God.

To Kierkegaard, Jesus was the absolute paradox because he became a man. God, the infinite and spiritual, became finite and temporal (of this world). Because reason cannot reconcile this life, Kierkegaard advocates accepting it on faith. For man to understand, he needs the teacher, but he also requires the condition for understanding it, and Kierkegaard maintains this condition is faith.

Faith, Kierkegaard says, is an individual choice. Contemporaries of Jesus faced the same difficulties as Kierkegaard's contemporaries faced (and we face today). What happened before is of no consequence: Everyone must make a choice.

In Philosophical Fragments, Kierkegaard offers that, when man is in error, he is in sin. He talks about the role of the teacher and guilt and atonement in this passage:

> What now shall we call such a Teacher, one who restores the lost condition and gives the learner Truth? . . . [L]et us call him *Redeemer,* for he redeems the learner from the captivity into which he had plunged himself, and no captivity is so terrible and so impossible to break, as that in which the individual keeps himself . . . by his self-imposed bondage the learner has brought upon himself a burden of guilt, and when the Teacher gives him the condition and the Truth he constitutes himself an *Atonement,* taking away the wrath impending upon that of which the learner has made himself guilty.

In *The Concept of Dread,* covered in the next chapter, he picks up this same theme and takes a look at original sin and guilt. In this book, Kierkegaard shows how freedom, sin, and dread are connected.

6 The Concept of Dread

It requires more courage to suffer than to act, more courage to forget than to remember, and perhaps the most wonderful thing about God is that he can forget man's sins.

—Søren Kierkegaard

The Concept of Dread is similar to other works by Kierkegaard: It is published under a pseudonym, it starts by reflecting on a Bible story, and it concerns itself with issues of faith. In this work, Kierkegaard tackles one of philosophy's and religion's thorniest issues—the role of sin in the world. How did sin enter the world? Why did God allow for sin? How can original sin still be relevant today?

Kierkegaard starts with the story of Adam and Eve and then traces the course of original (or hereditary) sin. From this reflection, he comes up with his definition of dread or anxiety. (You'll find other translations of this book's title; the original word is *Angest* and may be translated as "Anxiety" or "Anguish.") This chapter discusses this work, published in 1844, just days after *Philosophical Fragments*.

The Author, Vigilus Haufniensis

Kierkegaard published *The Concept of Dread* under the pseudonym Vigilus Haufniensis (which means "watchful (or alert) Copenhager" or, in other translations, "the night-watchman of Copenhagen"). Unlike Johannes Climacus (the pseudonym Kierkegaard used for *Philosophical Fragments*), this character is not associated with a real person. However, throughout his work, the various characters Kierkegaard creates maintain a certain consistent persona and writing style.

As in his other works, Kierkegaard does not speak directly to the author. Instead, he uses Haufniensis to present that character's point of view. The reader is left the task of understanding Haufniensis's (and therefore Kierkegaard's) thinking and then agreeing or disagreeing with the arguments he presents.

The Writing Style

The writing style of *The Concept of Dread* is similar to *Philosophical Fragments*. Like that work, *The Concept of Dread* is composed of five chapters and an introduction. The book can be difficult to read; some reviewers think this difficulty may have been the author's intent, which he himself likens anxiety to dizziness:

> Anxiety may be compared with dizziness. He whose eye happens to look down into the yawning abyss becomes dizzy. But what is the reason for this? It is just as much in his own eye in the abyss, for suppose he had not looked down. Hence anxiety is the dizziness of freedom, which emerges when the spirit wants to posit the synthesis and freedom looks down into its own possibility, laying hold of finiteness to support itself.

Reading and making sense of the difficult text may be intended to make the reader dizzy, to encounter the same feeling as anxiety itself brings out. Kierkegaard says that sin has its beginnings in anxiety, and he uses the story of Adam and Eve to illustrate his thoughts on sin.

Adam and Eve's First Sin

Original sin, in Biblical versions, entered the world after God created Adam and Eve. The creation and fall of man is described in Genesis. After God created man and woman, he placed only one restriction on them: "But of the tree of knowledge of good and evil, thou shalt not eat of it: for in the day that thou eatest thereof thou shalt surely die" (Genesis 2:16–17).

Eve is tempted by the snake, who tells her that if she eats fruit she won't die, but instead "your eyes shall be opened and ye shall be as gods, knowing good and evil" (Genesis 3:5). So Eve ate the fruit and then gave the fruit to Adam, who also ate the fruit. When they heard God, they hid themselves because they were ashamed, and God condemned them.

This original sin is passed down from generation to generation so that everyone is born into original or inherited sin. When Christ was born and then crucified, he redeemed believers from sin. According to Christianity, belief in Christ and his resurrection provides salvation from sin and eternal life.

Kierkegaard starts *The Concept of Dread* from this story and its problematic definition of sin, which he sums up as "sin entered the world through a sin." Kierkegaard seeks to recast the definition of sin. He starts by describing how sin should be considered.

Placing Sin in Its Place

Kierkegaard spends most of the first part of *The Concept of Dread* explaining where sin should fall as a topic to be studied. He titles his introduction "The Sense in which the Subject of our Deliberation is a Task of Psychological Interest and the Sense in which, after having been the Task and Interest of Psychology, it Points Directly to Dogmatics."

One reason he goes into this detailed analysis is that, in the prevailing view of the time (Hegel's System), there cannot be a "concept" of sin. He discusses why some of the many ways to categorize sin aren't accurate:

> Sin does not properly belong in any science, but it is the subject of the sermon, in which the single individual speaks to the single individual. In our day, scientific self-importance has tricked pastors into becoming something like professional clerks who also service science and find it beneath their dignity to preach.

He points out that sin has been studied from a metaphysical, ethical, and aesthetic viewpoint. And at the end of the Introduction, Kierkegaard summarizes his placement of sin—that is, why a psychological consideration fits:

> . . . [I]t is easily seen that the author is quite justified in calling the present work a psychological deliberation, and also how this deliberation, insofar as it becomes conscious of its relation to science, belongs to the domain of psychology and in turn tends toward dogmatics. Psychology has been called the doctrine of the subjective spirit. If this is pursued more accurately, it will become apparent how psychology, when it comes to the issue of sin, must first pass over into the doctrine of the absolute spirit. Here lies the place of dogmatics.

Because Kierkegaard is concerned that the study of sin may alter the outcome (that is, make the sin happen), he is very exact in his guidelines for sin's study, describing the mood appropriate for the study of sin. He pinpoints the psychological study at the moment "where it seems as if sin were there" but not beyond the moment that "sin is there." He states that these two states are "qualitatively different." For psychological study, "only the possibility of sin belongs to it." He states that "psychological observers need more agility than tightrope dancers; they must be able to incline and bend themselves towards others, imitating their postures; and their silence in the moment of intimacy should be both seductive and voluptuous."

From this precise background, he then presents his psychological deliberations on sin.

Sin from Ignorance

To understand sin, Kierkegaard starts with the idea that sin arises from innocence. Before the Fall, Adam did not know the difference between good and evil. Kierkegaard states, "Innocence is ignorance." He then connects innocence to anxiety or dread:

> In this state [innocence] there is peace and repose, but there is simultaneously something else that is not contention and strife, for there is indeed nothing against which to strive. What, then, is it? Nothing. But what effect does nothing have? It begets anxiety. This is the profound secret of innocence, that it is at the same time anxiety.

The Paradox of Sin

Kierkegaard focuses on choices and actions as the defining aspects of human character, and Adam and Eve both had the freedom to "choose" to disregard the directive of God and chose to "act" against this directive. Traditionally this is the answer to a longstanding question of original sin: If Adam and Eve didn't know the difference between good and evil, how can it have been a sin? And if it wasn't a sin, then how did God act justly by punishing them and all of humanity? The answer is that they made a choice and acted. Kierkegaard is well aware of this paradox.

Kierkegaard then goes on to define this anxiety in detail and explain how to deal with it.

Anxiety Defined

To Kierkegaard, "[A]nxiety is the possibility of freedom." He says that anxiety is "defined as freedom's disclosure to itself in possibility." Basically, Adam (who represents all people) dreads his freedom, his ability to choose. He dreads the possibilities that arise from his freedom. Because he is responsible for his actions and their consequences, Adam is afraid of what he might do, of what he is free to do. Kierkegaard writes, "[I]n possibility all things are equally possible, and whoever has been brought up by possibility has grasped the terrible as well as the joyful."

Kierkegaard also says that anxiety is a paradox; that is, "Dread is sympathetic antipathy and an antipathetic sympathy." This means that one wants what one fears and one fears what one wants. Kierkegaard writes in his journals:

> The nature of original sin has often been considered, and yet the principal category is missing—it is dread, that is what really determines it; for dread is a desire for what one fears, a sympathetic antipathy; dread is an alien power which takes hold of an individual, and yet one cannot extricate oneself from it, does not wish to, because one is afraid, but what one fears attracts one.

Anxiety and the Forbidden

Adam becomes aware of this freedom when God prohibits him from eating the fruit from the tree of knowledge. Adam does not know the difference between good and evil, nor does he know death. So he struggles to understand God's words:

> Because Adam has not understood what was spoken, there is nothing but the ambiguity of anxiety. The infinite possibility of being able that was awakened by the prohibition now draws closer, because this possibility points to a possibility as its sequence.

Innocence then becomes connected to the forbidden and punishment: "In anxiety it [innocence] is related to the forbidden and to the punishment. Innocence is not guilty, yet there is anxiety as though it were lost." God's prohibition brought about Adam's awareness of his ability to choose whether to follow God's rule; he knows he can disobey God if he wants. This realization makes him not only want to do so, but also dread doing so. He is anxious about the possibility and his freedom in determining the actual from the possible.

Anxiety of the Future

In his description of anxiety, Kierkegaard also explains how anxiety is particularly tied to the future. He says, "For freedom, the possibility is the future, and the future is for time the possible. To both of these corresponds anxiety in the individual." He shows how, if someone is anxious, that anxiety is always related to the future:

> If I am anxious about a past misfortune, then this is not because it is in the past but because it may be repeated, i.e., become future. If I am anxious because of a past offense, it is because I have not placed it an essential relation to myself as past and have in some deceitful way or other presented it from being past. If indeed it is actually past, then I cannot be anxious but only repentant. If I do not repent, I have allowed myself to make my relation to the offense dialectical, and by this the offense itself has become a possibility and not something past.

In this way, anxiety is also about nothing (the same nothing that preceded the Fall). The future is not real; it is nothing. Because the future is not defined and because an individual must create his or her own future, dread is also fear of this responsibility—making choices that define that person's life.

Anxiety for All

Kierkegaard also elaborates on the presence of anxiety (and sin) in everyone's life. He discusses the moment that Adam sinned and reminds the reader that everyone faces this same moment: "the moment is there for Adam as well for every subsequent individual." People can't blame Adam for sin because sin is always tied to an individual:

> For sin is precisely the transcendence, the *discrimem rerum* [critical moment] through which sin enters into a single individual as a single individual. Sin never comes into the world differently, nor has it ever done so. So when a single individual is foolish enough to ask about sin as if it were irrelevant to him, he asks only a fool.

In that same chapter, he writes that the common people realize "that it was not just six thousand years ago that sin came into the world." Instead, sin should be the concern for each individual personally. "How sin came into the world, each of us can understand for ourselves; if we try to learn it from someone else, we will *eo ipso* misunderstand it."

Kierkegaard stresses the individual and the individual's responsibility to choose. That is, anxiety is relevant to everyone. About the progress from anxiety to faith, Kierkegaard says

. . . it is an adventure that every human being must go through—to learn to be anxious in order that he may not perish either by never having been in anxiety or by succumbing to anxiety. Whoever has learned to be anxious in the right way has learned the ultimate.

Kierkegaard writes even more on anxiety. He maintains that the greater the man, the greater the anxiety: "[T]he more profoundly he is in anxiety, the greater is the man." Also, he underlines the idea that man is ultimately responsible for that anxiety. Although man may want to think that "anxiety is about something external, about something outside a person," Kierkegaard states that man "himself produces the anxiety."

Kierkegaard then provides his version of how to learn to be anxious in "the right way."

Faith and Anxiety

Kierkegaard's criticism of other philosophers—Hegel, for instance—was that they talked about abstract concepts and theories but didn't really tell people how to live or how to deal with the problems resulting from these abstractions. Kierkegaard maintained that what he really needed to know was what he must do, not what he must know. He backs up this opinion in *The Concept of Dread* by providing a view of how to live, particularly how to deal with anxiety.

He says that "possibility can be educative" and states that "he who passes through the anxiety of the possible is educated to have no anxiety, not because he can escape the terrible things of life but because these always become weak by comparison with those of possibility." Anxiety can have a transformative power: It can make you aware that you are free to choose.

Kierkegaard stresses the importance of faith: "If at the beginning of his education he misunderstands the anxiety, so that it does not lead him to faith but away from faith, then he is lost." Kierkegaard says that, with faith, one is equipped to handle the anxiety: "[S]uch anxiety is through faith absolutely educative, because it consumes all finite ends and discovers all their deceptiveness."

In *The Concept of Dread,* Kierkegaard uses the analogy of a hypochondriac to show how what someone worries about in general is worse than any particular outcome:

The hypochondriac is anxious about every insignificant thing, but when the significant appears he begins to breathe more easily. And why?

Because the significant actuality is not after all so terrible as the possibility he himself has fashioned, and which he used his strength to fashion, whereas he can now use all his strength against actuality.

By becoming and remaining aware of the possibility of sinning, by being "sin-conscious," an individual will not get rid of anxiety, but learn to welcome it and use it for a purpose:

> . . . [W]hoever is educated [by possibility] remains with anxiety; he does not permit himself to be deceived by its countless falsifications. . . . Then the assaults of anxiety, even though they be terrifying, will not be such that he flees from them. For him, anxiety becomes a serving spirit that against its will leads him where he wishes to go.

He repeats this same idea later when he writes, "[A]nxiety enters into his soul and searches out everything and anxiously torments everything finite and petty out of him, and then it leads him where he wants to go." He also writes that "when the individual through anxiety is educated unto faith, anxiety will eradicate precisely what it brings forth itself."

Themes in The Concept of Dread

The Concept of Dread concerns itself with the origins of sin. From his ponderings on sin, Kierkegaard says that Adam was in anxiety when faced with his freedom. Anxiety is not sin itself and does not necessarily lead to sin. Adam—and everyone else who has lived since Adam—had a choice. When Adam chose to eat the fruit, he took a leap from freedom to sin. Likewise, each individual makes the same leap. Choosing sin not only compounds the anxiety but also provides the opportunity to return to God (to leap back to God through faith).

Like his other writings, readers can see the influence of Kierkegaard's religious upbringing. Sin and suffering, as well as the idea of sins of the father being passed on to the son, are prevalent.

This work, like others, continues Kierkegaard's quest to learn how to be a Christian in Christendom. Kierkegaard highlights faith as the saving grace. He uses again the leap, here from freedom to sin and then possibly from sin back to God (through faith). He goes against the prevailing philosophy of his time; he doesn't think that reason is always supreme or even relevant—for instance, with matters of faith.

In addition, in *The Concept of Dread* readers can see Kierkegaard's emphasis on the individual and individual choices as well as his belief that truth is subjective. These existential themes are later picked up by other philosophers.

Kierkegaard didn't use the term *existential* to define his work, but he is acknowledged as the Father of Existentialism. *The Concept of Dread*, in particular, is a work that influenced other existential philosophers, including the French existential philosopher Jean-Paul Sartre (1905–1980), Martin Heidegger (1889–1976), Albert Camus (1913–1960), Karl Jaspers (1883–1969), and many others. The terms Kierkegaard uses, such as *existence, freedom, responsibility,* and *anxiety* or *anguish,* are concepts other existential philosophers used and elaborated on in their works. Sartre, for instance, says, "We are condemned to be free."

In *Concluding Unscientific Postscript,* Kierkegaard adds to and clarifies the concepts he presented in *Philosophical Fragments.* This book is the topic of the next chapter.

7 Concluding Unscientific Postscript

It is the duty of the human understanding to understand that there are things which it cannot understand, and what those things are.

—Søren Kierkegaard

Concluding Unscientific Postscript was published in February 1846 and took up where *Philosophical Fragments* left off. This work is the culmination of many of Kierkegaard's major themes and is his most recognized work of "existential" thought. *Concluding Unscientific Postscript* presents a criticism of Hegel's System, the idea that truth is subjective, the importance of the individual, the role of faith versus reason as it relates to religious truth, the acceptance of paradoxical concepts, how to be, and the difficulties of being a Christian.

Although Kierkegaard did write from a Christian point of view, his work is not relevant only to Christians. His work contains themes, issues, and concepts that are relevant today. In fact, many of his existential concepts have been read and promoted by atheist and agnostic philosophers.

This chapter provides an overview of the parts of *Concluding Unscientific Postscript* and its pseudonymous author, and then discusses the key concepts and themes.

The Author and Structure of Concluding Unscientific Postscript

Concluding Unscientific Postscript was written under the pseudonym Johannes Climacus, the same pseudonym Kierkegaard used for *Philosophical*

Fragments. (Chapter 5 discusses the significance of this pseudonym.) In *Concluding Unscientific Postscript,* Kierkegaard continues the theme of religious truth that he started in *Philosophical Fragments.* In *Philosophical Fragments,* he writes that "[t]he idea of demonstrating that this unknown something [God] exists, could scarcely suggest itself to Reason. For if God does not exist it would of course be impossible to prove it, and if he does exist it would be folly to attempt it."

Although *Concluding Unscientific Postscript* was written as a "postscript" to *Philosophical Fragments,* it is actually much, much longer than the earlier work. The title is a knock to Hegel's System. (Hegel's goal was a comprehensive system of thought, and although he did not complete this work, he thought that his followers would soon finish up by adding a few "postscripts.")

The book includes many goals and explores many theses; it is composed of several chapters, appendixes, and additions:

- The goal of the first part of the book is to discuss the objective problem of whether Christianity is true. This part contains two main sections: "The Historical Point of View" and "The Speculative Point of View." Kierkegaard offers the end result that Christianity cannot be proved (or disproved) historically or speculatively.

- The second part of the book tackles the concept of subjective truth and the relationship of the individual to Christianity. This part includes two sections. In the first section, Kierkegaard pulls four theses from Lessing, another philosopher, and uses them to comment on subjectivity, the limits of Hegel's System, and direct and indirect communication. In the second section, he offers advice on "becoming subjective."

- The chapter "Actual Ethical Subjectivity" criticizes the disinterestedness of people and the role of ethics in subjectivity.

- Kierkegaard includes a chapter that is a summary of *Philosophical Fragments,* yet this summary is longer than that book. This summary includes Part A, a definition of "existential pathos," and Part B, the contradictions between eternal truth and historical fact.

- The Conclusion describes the difficulty of becoming a Christian and uses the story of the mistaken highway robber to comment on truth.

A robber puts on a wig, robs a traveler, and then discards the wig. A poor man finds the wig, puts it on, and is arrested for the robbery of the traveler. The real robber is in court and tells the judge, "It seems that the traveler has regard rather to the wig than to the man." He tries on the wig, and the traveler then recognizes him as the robber, but the traveler has already sworn it was the poor man. Kierkegaard ends the conclusion with this:

So it is, in one way or another, with every man who has a "what" and is not attentive to the "how": he swears, he takes his oath, he runs errands, he ventures life and blood, he is executed—all on account of the wig.

- Kierkegaard includes an Appendix that he titles "Towards an Understanding of My Reader." He describes himself as essentially a comedic writer in this piece.

- The Appendix isn't the last piece; Kierkegaard then includes another section, titled "First and Last Explanation." In this piece, he lists his pseudonymous works and confesses he is the author of them.

Problems with Hegel and Rationalism

One of the main thrusts of *Concluding Unscientific Postscript* is the criticism of Hegel's System. Kierkegaard takes issue with this prevailing philosophy because it is incomplete and because Hegel writes from outside the System. He questions where and how the System was begun.

In this criticism, Kierkegaard doesn't just attack Hegel but raises issues with the emphasis on rationalism. Kierkegaard didn't just disagree with Hegel's System; he disagreed with any systematic approach to knowledge. In this regard, *Concluding Unscientific Postscript* was a turning point in philosophy. Kierkegaard offered a new approach and new ideas.

This section discusses the points Kierkegaard makes in his critique of Hegel's System.

Hegel's System

In short, Hegel created what he thought was a comprehensive system of thought based on reason or abstraction. He offers an evolutionary view of human reason; that is, man moves from levels of truth until he eventually arrives at the absolute truth. In Hegel's view, God is this Absolute Truth. God, then, becomes immanent, all that exists.

Man is defined in relation to others, and his greatest good is as part of society. Hegel emphasizes the whole rather than the individual. Kierkegaard takes issue with all these assertions.

The Incomplete System

In his criticism, Kierkegaard mocks the System because it is not complete. In *Concluding Unscientific Postscript,* he writes, "Tell me now sincerely, is it entirely finished; for if so I will kneel down before it, even at the risk of ruining a pair of trousers (for on account of the heavy traffic to and from the system, the road has become quite muddy)." In other words, if the truth is in the whole, how can the System be true if it's not complete, not whole?

This passage shows Kierkegaard's use of humor to make his point about the incompleteness of the System. He also asserts that experience is never complete; therefore, how could a system of thought be complete?

Where Does the System Start?

Kierkegaard also questions where and how the System started: "How does the System begin with the immediate [given]? That is to say, does it begin with it immediately?" He asks, "With what do I begin, now that I have abstracted everything? . . . [W]ith nothing. And it is indeed true, as the system says, that it begins with nothing. . . . How do I begin with nothing?" Kierkegaard points out the flaws in the System's logic and its main tenets.

Outside Looking In

In Hegel's System, the thinker (Hegel) is outside the System; Kierkegaard exposes where this thinking eventually leads: "But who is this systematic thinker? . . . It is he who is outside of existence and yet in existence, who is in his eternity forever complete, and yet includes all existence within himself—it is God." He criticizes Hegel for taking the role of God in the System. Kierkegaard also points out the inherent weakness in a system where the thinker is outside the system.

The Problem with Abstractions

Kierkegaard also points out the problems with the reliance on reason or abstraction. He writes, "Abstract thinking is conducted sub specie æterni [from the point of view of eternity], and therefore disregards the concrete and the temporal, the becoming of existence." He compares using abstraction or pure thought this way: "Existing under the guidance of pure thought is like traveling through Denmark and relying on a small map of Europe, on which Denmark is no larger than a dot."

In *Concluding Unscientific Postscript,* Kierkegaard uses irony, humor, and logic to make his points. He jokes, "I assume that anyone I may have honor to talk with is also a human being. If he presumes to be speculative philosophy in the abstract, pure speculative thought, I must renounce the effort to speak with him; for in that case he instantly vanishes from my sight."

Hegel's System puts everything in its place and, thus, destroys the role of possibility, of having and making choices. Kierkegaard asserts that a man's choices define his actions and his life; therefore, having possibilities and making choices is critical. He offers another view of truth, truth as subjective.

Truth Is Subjectivity

Kierkegaard famously said, "Truth is subjectivity," and in *Concluding Unscientific Postscript,* he contrasts objective and subjective truth. He stresses that objective truth has no relevance in issues of ethics and religion and that the real truth is what's true for the individual. Subjective truth, truth that is related to one's experience and values, is what affects a person and motivates actions and decisions. Kierkegaard makes several points about subjective truth, summarized in this section.

Communicating Subjectivity

Kierkegaard discusses objectivity and subjectivity as they relate to communication and asserts that subjectivity can only be communicated indirectly (this is the first thesis in the second part of the book). Of objective thinking he says

> Objective thinking is completely indifferent to subjectivity and therefore to inwardness and inward appropriation; its method of communication is therefore direct. . . . It can be understood directly and reeled off by rote, is aware only of itself, so it is not really communication at all.

Because "direct communication demands certainty, but certainty is impossible for anyone in a process of becoming," Kierkegaard says that "those who try to communicate it [truth] directly are therefore fools, and so are those who expect them to do so."

In the second thesis, he describes the opposites of being and nonbeing and assigns the terms *negative* and *positive.* He aligns subjective thought with negative thought because it considers the "nothingness which pervades existence," and existence is meaningful only when weighed against that "nothingness."

Categories of thought that objectively seem true, Kierkegaard maintains, are not:

> Positivity can be classified under the following categories: sense-certainty, historical knowledge, and speculative result . . . sense-certainty is deceptive . . . historical knowledge is illusionary . . . and the speculative results are a muddled mishmash.

This type of knowledge may provide facts about the world, but it provides nothing on how to live and is, in Kierkegaard's view, less important.

The What and How

Kierkegaard contrasts objective and subjective thought with what each emphasizes: *"The objective accent falls on WHAT is said, the subjective accent on HOW it is said."* Because there is no way to validate or prove anything, the passions—the how of one's beliefs—"constitute the truth." He uses the following example to illustrate his point:

> If one who lives in the midst of Christianity goes up to the house of God, the house of the true God, with the true conception of God in his knowledge and prays, but prays in a false spirit; and one who lives in an idolatrous community prays with the entire passion of the infinite, although his eyes rest upon the image of an idol: where is the most truth? The one prays in truth to God though he worships an idol; the other prays falsely to the true God, and hence worships in fact an idol.

He explains subjectivity as it relates to the knowledge of God:

> Objectively, reflection is directed to the problem of whether this object is in the true God; subjectively, reflection is directed to the question whether the individual is related to a something *in such a manner* that his relationship is in truth a God-relationship.

The relationship and its truth is what is valid. He continues his arguments for subjective truth and, in doing so, defines existence, the topic of the next section.

The Definition of Existence

To Kierkegaard, existence was always in flux, in what he calls "the constant process of becoming," and in the state of becoming, nothing was predestined or determined. He writes, "The perpetual process of becoming is in the uncertainty of earthly life, where everything is uncertain." He compares the Socratic position that "the knower is an existing individual, and that the task of existing is his essential task" to the process of becoming:

> Existing subjective thinkers are constantly striving; but this does not mean that they have a finite goal, and that their striving will be finished when they reach it, for they strive infinitely in a constant process of becoming.

Experience is never complete; no person is ever complete. To exist means a constant striving for a goal that is infinite. Because of this, Kierkegaard maintains that existence can't be abstracted. You cannot think existence; you must live it.

Kierkegaard uses Lessing's idea of truth and striving (his fourth thesis in the second part of *Concluding Unscientific Postscript*):

> Lessing said: If God were holding complete truth in his right hand and in his left a singular and always restless striving after the truth, a striving in which I would err for ever and a day, and if he directed me to choose between them, I would humbly ask for his left hand and say, Father grant me this, for pure truth belongs to you alone.

Kierkegaard agrees that truth belongs to God alone, and he shows how objective thought does not include ethics, another problem.

Ethics and Abstraction

Kierkegaard includes a section that talks about the ethics (or lack of ethics) in abstraction. He writes

> . . . the Hegelian philosophy goes on and becomes an existential system in sheer distraction of mind, and what is more, is finished—without

having an Ethics (where existence properly belongs)—the more simple philosophy which is propounded by an existing individual for existing individuals, will more especially emphasize the ethical.

He criticizes abstract thought for raising a person above temporal concerns into "pure being" and equating abstract thought with the highest type of thinking:

> We must therefore be wary of abstract thinkers and their wish to remain for ever in the pure being of abstraction, which they regard as the highest of human attainments, while abstract thought—which leads to neglect of the ethical and misunderstanding of the religious—is treated as the highest form of human thinking.

In contrast, a subjective thinker is not deceived and realizes the incompleteness of existence, as well as the striving and learning required:

> In the ethical sense, on the contrary, the persistent striving represents the consciousness of being an existing individual: the constant learning is the expression of this incessant realization, in no moment complete as long as the subject is in existence; the subject is aware of this fact, and hence is not deceived.

Kierkegaard also stresses the individual and his or her choices, the "I" versus the non-defined "we." He writes that "the ethical is concerned with particular human beings, and with each and every one of them by himself." He denounces going along with and hiding in the crowd, another existential theme.

The Crowd versus The Individual

Because abstract thinking does not make an individual accountable, Kierkegaard decries how easy it is to pay lip service to concepts, but not truly live them. He says that the problems with objective thinking would have been "realized long ago if pure thought had not been borne up by an awe-inspiring public reputation, so that no one would dare question its magnificence, or admit that they do not understand it." He illustrates how a person will go along with the crowd "because he is afraid of what acquaintances and neighbors will think of him if he does not agree to its validity."

He summarizes being part of the crowd compared to being an individual with this passage: "Being an individual man is a thing that has been abolished, and every speculative philosopher confuses himself with humanity at large, whereby he becomes something infinitely great—and at the same time nothing at all."

These ideas echo thoughts he included in his journals. About the majority and truth he writes in his journals:

> Truth always rests with the minority, and the minority is always stronger than the majority, because the minority is generally formed by those who really have an opinion, while the strength of a majority is illusory, formed by the gangs who have no opinion—and who, therefore, in the next instant (when it is evident that the minority is the stronger) assume its opinion . . . while Truth again reverts to a new minority.

Kierkegaard especially stresses the individual before God. In his journals, he again writes

> Spiritual superiority only sees the individual. But alas, ordinarily we human beings are sensual and, therefore, as soon as it is a gathering, the impression changes—we see something abstract, the crowd, and we become different. But in the eyes of God, the infinite spirit, all the millions that have lived and now live do not make a crowd, He only sees each individual.

Becoming Subjective

Kierkegaard doesn't just criticize the existing thought; he also provides a way to live differently. Kierkegaard's goal throughout his career was to learn to be Christian, and he ties subjective truth to Christianity (although this does not make it relevant to Christianity alone). He writes that "philosophy teaches the way to become objective, while Christianity teaches that the way is to become subjective, i.e. to become a subject in truth." He claims that "Christianity protests every form of objectivity; it desires that the subject should be infinitely concerned about himself."

He stresses the individual, subjective thinker and Christianity's potential transformation with this passage:

> Christianity proposes to endow the individual with an eternal happiness, a good which is not distributed wholesale, but only to one individual at a time. Though Christianity assumes that there inheres in the subjectivity of the individual, as being the potentiality of the appropriation of this good, the possibility for its acceptance, it does not assume

that the subjectivity is immediately ready for such acceptance or even that it has, without further ado, a real conception of the significance of such a good.

Each person has the potential for goodness, even if he is not aware of it or even the value of that goodness. Kierkegaard elaborates on the tasks required to become subjective, to become a Christian.

What Is a Christian?

Kierkegaard asks what it means to become a Christian and offers several possible responses. Is it the acceptance of the doctrine of Christianity? Is it the diligence in which one holds fast to the doctrine? Is it determined by what one has undergone (in particular, baptism)? He responds with the ineffectiveness of doctrines to define belief:

> Christianity is no doctrine concerning the unity of the divine and the human, or concerning the identity of the subject and object; nor is it any other of the logical transcriptions of Christianity. . . . Christianity is therefore not a doctrine, but the fact that God has existed.

And he counters all the other possibilities and in the end concludes "the thing of being a Christian is not determined by the *what* of Christianity but by the *how* of the Christian."

Accepting Paradoxes

He returns to previous themes of the paradox inherent in religion and discusses the particular paradox of Jesus, of the temporal and eternal existing together: "The absurd is—that the eternal truth has come into being in time, that God has come into being, has been born, has grown up, and so forth, has come into being precisely like any other individual human being."

Instead of using reason or abstractions to explain the paradox (which is impossible), Kierkegaard advocates simply accepting them. Kierkegaard isn't against reason; he simply maintains that reason has no role in religious belief. He offers that when faced with a paradox, a person can take offense or believe because of and in spite of the absurdity of the paradox. This is where faith comes in: "with truth confronting the individual as a paradox, gripped in the anguish and pain of sin, facing the tremendous risk of the objective insecurity, the individual believes." Kierkegaard goes on to say that "[f]or the absurd is the object of faith, and the only object that can be believed" and "the object of faith is thus God's reality in existence as a particular individual, the fact that God has existed as an individual human being."

Existentialism Beginnings

This work also highlights the existentialism rejection of the mindset that knowledge must be grounded in reason or rationality. The reader sees a shift of concern or emphasis away from "knowing" to "being." To Kierkegaard, reason is useless and provides no knowledge of Christianity (or any kind of subjective experience). His approach doesn't dismiss empirical data, but suggests a different way to evaluate subjective experience.

The Role of Faith

One of Kierkegaard's criticisms of Hegel's System is that, if everything is known, why does one need faith? Instead, Kierkegaard not only believed in the importance of faith, but said that faith has its truth in subjectivity. He writes that "faith inheres in subjectivity" and describes the risk involved in believing:

> Without risk there is no faith. Faith is precisely the contraction between the infinite passion of the individual's inwardness and the subjective uncertainty. If I am capable of grasping God objectively, I do not believe, but precisely because I cannot do this I must believe.

Kierkegaard offers this definition of faith: *"Faith is the objective uncertainty along with the repulsion of the absurd held fast in the passion of inwardness, which precisely is inwardness potentiated to the highest degree."* He states that "passion is man's perdition, but it is his exaltation as well."

But what about the person who believes in idols? What about the person who believes wrongly, even if passionately? Kierkegaard says that, if a person has true passion, he or she will ultimately be led to the truth. He claims that "he who with quiet introspection is honest before God and concerned for himself, the Deity saves from being in error . . . him the Deity leads by the suffering of inwardness to the truth."

The Difficulty in Existing in Truth

Kierkegaard knows, though, that "to exist in truth, so that our existence becomes saturated with consciousness—to be eternal, as if far beyond existence, at the same time as being present in it and yet in the process of becoming—that really is difficult." In the section "The Religious Task: an Edifying Divertissement," Kierkegaard talks about how a sermon is understood "with such fearful ease" on Sunday, but on "Monday it is very difficult to understand that it concerns this little particular within the relative and concrete existence in which the individual has his daily life." He talks about the difficulty in putting words and ideas into action: "[T]he clergyman speaks in general terms about the innocent pleasures of life, but you have to express existentially what the clergyman says."

He also considers that living this way requires making decisions and how tempting it is to avoid decisions (and thus responsibilities): "the more difficult the matter becomes, the greater the temptation to hasten along the easy road of speculation, away from fearful dangers and crucial decisions." He also acknowledges the status afforded reason and abstract thinking. He says "to think about the simple things of life . . . is extremely forbidding . . . thinking about the high-falutin is very much more attractive and glorious."

But Kierkegaard says that the struggle is worth it:

> Nature, the totality of created things, is the work of God. And yet God is not there; but within the individual man there is a potentiality (man is potentially spirit) which is awakened in inwardness to become a God-relationship, and then it becomes possible to see God everywhere.

Kierkegaard's Role as Author

In addition to elaborating on truth, *Concluding Unscientific Postscript* also includes several elements about Kierkegaard as an author. In the Appendix to the work, titled "An Understanding with my Reader," and in the piece after that, "A First and Last Explanation," Kierkegaard calls himself essentially a humorist, confesses he is the author of his pseudonymous works, and explains his reasoning for this type of authorship. He claims he used a pseudonym not for legal reasons or on a personal whim. Instead, he says his method of indirect communication "is *essential* to the nature of my output itself."

He cautions his readers not to confuse him with his poetized authors and says, "What I have written is therefore undeniably mine, but only in so far as I have put a life-view into the mouth of a poetically actual creative individual by making his words audible." He stresses the need of the reader to create his own meaning:

The poetized author has his own definite life-view, but views which may be meaningful, witty and refreshing when understood in that way might sound strange, ludicrous or even repulsive in the mouth of some single, definite, real individual.

Kierkegaard was a prolific author, a brilliant and creative wordsmith, a critic of philosophy and theology, the father of existential thought. In summary, he became an individual.

Further Reading

Kierkegaard's Books

The Concept of Anxiety (or *The Concept of Dread*)

The Concept of Irony

Concluding Unscientific Postscript

Either/Or

Fear and Trembling

The Journals of Kierkegaard

Philosophical Fragments

The Point of View for My Work as an Author

Practice in Christianity

Repetition

The Sickness Unto Death

Stages on Life's Way

Works of Love

Anthologies

Bretall, Robert, ed. *A Kierkegaard Anthology*. Princeton: Princeton University Press, 1946.

Chamberlain, Jane and Jonathan Ree, eds. *The Kierkegaard Reader*. Oxford: Blackwell Publishers, 2001.

Hong, Edward and Edna Hong, eds. *The Essential Kierkegaard*. Princeton: Princeton University Press, 2000.

Biographies and Critical Works

Gardiner, Patrick. *Kierkegaard: A Very Short Introduction.* Oxford: Oxford University Press, 1988.

Hannay, Alastair and Gordon D. Marino, eds. *The Cambridge Companion to Kierkegaard.* Cambridge: Cambridge University Press, 1998.

Robinson, Dave and Oscar Zarate. *Introducing Kierkegaard.* Cambridge: Icon Books, 2003.

Kierkegaard Web Sites

Dr. Anthony Storm's Commentary on Kierkegaard. www.soren kierkegaard.org. — Contains a biography of Kierkegaard, a primer on Kierkegaardian motifs, and information about his authorial method.

Kierkegaard on the Internet. www.webcom.com/kierke. — Includes a biography, a chronology of Kierkegaard's life and work, and several pages called "Writer and Thinker" that discuss many of Kierkegaard's works.

Philosophy Pages from Garth Kemerling. www. philosophypages.com. — Contains a biography and a detailed bibliography of works by and about Kierkegaard.

St. Olaf College Kierkegaard. www.stolaf.edu/collections/ kierkegaard. — Describes the library that contains many of Kierkegaard's works. Also lists special events and publications relating to Kierkegaard.

Søren Kierkegaard: Life and Work by F. J. Billeskov Jansen. www.denmark.org/culture/in_dk_literature_kierk. html. — A concise (ten pages or so) description of Kierkegaard's life and works.

The Kierkegaarden by Rosemarie Pena. www.heartrose.com/ gaarden. — Contains quotations from Kierkegaard's works.

General Philosophy

Magee, Bryan. *The Story of Philosophy.* London: Dorling Kindersley, 1998.

EpistemeLinks.com: Philosophy Resources on the Internet. www.epistemelinks.com. — Includes more than 15,000 categorized links to philosophy resources on the Internet.

Stanford Encyclopedia of Philosophy, edited by Edward N. Zalta. http://plato.stanford.edu. — An online version of the *Stanford Encyclopedia of Philosophy* with entries on philosophers, philosophy movements, and philosophical concepts.

Index